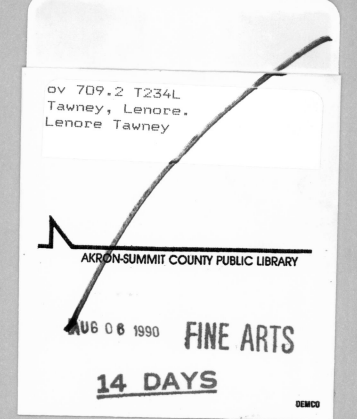

Lenore Tawney

A Retrospective

Lenore Tawney

A Retrospective

KATHLEEN NUGENT MANGAN, EDITOR

Color Photographs by George Erml

AMERICAN CRAFT MUSEUM
New York

RIZZOLI
NEW YORK

© 1959.
Yousuf Karsh

Published in conjunction with the exhibition
"Lenore Tawney: A Retrospective."

First published in the United States of America by Rizzoli
International Publications Inc.
300 Park Avenue South, New York, New York 10010

Library of Congress Cataloging-in-publication Data

Tawney, Lenore.
    Lenore Tawney : a retrospective : American Craft Museum,
New York
    Kathleen Nugent Mangan, editor ; color photographs by
George Erml.
        p.   cm.
    Includes bibliographical references.
    1. Tawney, Lenore—Exhibitions. I. Mangan, Kathleen
Nugent.
    II. Erml, George.   III. American Craft Museum (New York,
N.Y.)
    IV. Title.
    N6537.T38A4   1990
709'.2—dc20   89-43562
                CIP

ISBN 0–8478–1168–9
ISBN 0–8478–1169–7 (pbk.)

Design by Beth Tondreau Design

Jacket collage by Lenore Tawney, October, 1989

Set in type by David E. Seham Associates, Metuchen, New Jersey
Printed and bound by Toppan Printing Company, Tokyo, Japan

Contents

EXHIBITION SCHEDULE

American Craft Museum
April 18–June 21, 1990

Art Institute of Chicago
July 26–October 28, 1990

Renwick Gallery of the National Museum of American Art,
Smithsonian Institution, Washington, D.C.
April 12–July 21, 1991

This exhibition, the second in the "Master Artist" series, has been made possible through generous grants from the Henry Luce Foundation, The First National Bank of Chicago, the National Endowment for the Arts, a federal agency, and the New York State Council on the Arts.

Lenore Tawney in her South Street studio, working on *Vespers*, 1961.

Acknowledgments

Lenore Tawney was a major force in redefining postwar weaving. By inventing the means to free weaving from the boundaries of the loom, she created fiber sculpture that hangs freely in space. She also subverted the warp/weft grid when she released the edges from conventional alignment and allowed them to undulate away from or toward each other. These breakthroughs in fiber technique were seminal interventions in the history of textiles; they also emerged alongside certain pioneering efforts in painting and sculpture. As Tawney's inventions were releasing tapestry from the wall, the scale or format of concurrent sculpture was rendering the pedestal obsolete. While sculptors enlisted the physical presence of aluminum and steel in monumental structures to command the space in which they were viewed, Tawney employed fiber as a powerful distraction from the current fascination with industrial materials. She also mastered grand scale.

Tawney's incorporation of language aligns her work with a ubiquitous leitmotiv in twentieth-century art. Fragments from books in many languages enter her collages and constructions; fiber sculpture, created by the manipulation of threads, is a harmonious vehicle for an artist so enraptured with the linear contortions of language. Tawney's agile thread might also be considered in the same context as Agnes Martin's elusive pencil line.

Tawney's spiritual flight is fueled by a liaison with organic fragments. She weaves, hypnotized by the gestures of her own hand, benevolently ruled by her materials. Feathers, shells, eggs, stones introduced into a Tawney construction or collage convey a spiritual message that transcends their common origins or diminutive scale; the tiniest fragment of nature, in Tawney's hands, is endowed with content, with symbolism, with spirituality. One is tempted to consider the relationship of her constructions, many of them boxlike in shape, to those of Joseph Cornell.

Tawney's work reflects certain critical issues in sculpture but is particularly important because she has also merged extraordinary craft techniques with monumental scale. She depends upon an ancient medium while exploring radically new formats. One of the major figures in the fiber movement of the 1950s and 1960s, she has continued to make powerful statements in fiber as well as in her collages and constructions. Tawney's significant entry belongs not just in the craft continuum but in the history of late twentieth-century art.

THE AMERICAN CRAFT MUSEUM is honored to present the first comprehensive retrospective of the works of Lenore Tawney as the second in its series of exhibitions devoted to American masters. The requirements of such a major project as this exhibition and its accompanying publication could not have been met without the vision, support, and efforts of many. It must first be noted that neither the exhibition nor the catalogue could have become a reality without the generous support of the foundation, corporate, and public communities. We are especially grateful to the Henry Luce Foundation, Inc., The First National Bank of Chicago, the National Endowment for the Arts, and the New York State Council on the Arts. The lenders to the exhibition have our profound gratitude: The Art Institute of Chicago; Edna S. Beron; The Cleveland Museum of Art; Alex and Camille Cook; Cooper-Hewitt National Museum of Design, Smithsonian Institution, New York; Diana Epstein and Millicent Safro; the Art Collection of The First National Bank of Chicago; Ted Hallman; Katharine Kuh; The Metropolitan Museum of Art, New York; The Museum of Modern Art, New York; Philip Morris Companies, Inc.; Mrs. Jack Weinberg; and an anonymous lender. They have extended their loans so that this exhibition may travel to other museums. At those museums we wish to thank Christa C. Mayer Thurman, curator, department of textiles, and James N. Wood, director, the Art Institute of Chicago, and Michael W. Monroe, curator-in-charge, Renwick Gallery of the National Museum of American Art, Smithsonian Institution, Washington, D.C.

Exhibitions are short-lived; catalogues endure to enter history. The important documentation of this exhibition is greatly enhanced by the contributions of Dr. Erika Billeter, director of the Musée Cantonal des Beaux-Arts, Lausanne, Switzerland; Katharine Kuh; and Paul J. Smith, director emeritus, American Craft Museum, who conceived this exhibition. We are grateful also to Johanna Sophia, who translated the Billeter essay. Kathleen Nugent Mangan, as curator, has written the brilliant lead essay and elicited the contributions of all the authors.

The publication has been enriched by the respon-sive photographs of Tawney's work by George Erml. Gerald Zeigerman has served as our diligent and thoughtful editor. Solveig Williams, vice president, international rights and co-editions, and Sarah Burns, associate editor, at Rizzoli International Publications committed themselves to an excellent publication from our earliest discussions. Beth Tondreau conceived the complementary design of the catalogue.

To the following, who lent their good counsel, assisted with research, or helped us locate works, we express our appreciation: Elaine Benson, Helen Drutt English, Reverend E. S. Gault, Miani Johnson, Ruth Kaufmann, Ida Miller, Fern Moran, John Hallmark Neff, and Joyce Pomeroy Schwartz.

The board of governors of the American Craft Museum, under the visionary stewardship of Charles D. Peebler, Jr., chairman, has my abiding gratitude for the confidence and support bestowed so graciously upon this project.

The staff of the American Craft Museum has shown a tireless commitment. Although everyone has participated, particular thanks must be extended to Nina Stritzler, assistant curator, who attended to the myriad details of the exhibition and its catalogue with remarkable devotion. Invaluable assistance has also been provided by Frances Kelly, coordinator of traveling exhibitions; Elisabeth Massey, development associate; Joan McDonald, public relations officer; Robin Richenaker, assistant to the director; Doris Stowens, registrar; Virginia Strull, chief development officer; Scott VanderHamm, assistant registrar; and Anthea Zonars, assistant curator. Lois Moran, executive director of the American Craft Council, has our appreciation as well.

The penultimate acknowledgment is due Kathleen Nugent Mangan, the curator of this splendid exhibition. Her dedication, tactful persistence, and energetic efforts have been astonishing to witness. Thanks to her, we now can understand the significance of Tawney's contribution.

On behalf of Kathleen Nugent Mangan, I express her appreciation, as well as my own, to Lenore Tawney for her cooperation throughout the organization of the project, for the loan of her works, and espe-

Jacket collage by Lenore Tawney, October, 1989.

cially for sharing her private journals. Our final and therefore most important remarks are directed to the artist. We are all very grateful for the privilege of knowing her. It is Tawney's wisdom, unremitting search for perfection, courage, and unique talents that have given us the challenge, the inspiration, the pleasure, and the wonder of her work.

Lenore Tawney wishes to acknowledge ''with deepest appreciation and love'' her meditation teachers, Swami Muktananda and Swami Chidvilasananda.

JANET KARDON
Director
American Craft Museum

Foreword

KATHARINE KUH

The art of Lenore Tawney is multifaceted—yet all of one piece. A personal, hidden poetry transfuses it, whether the medium is fiber, collage, assemblage, or postcard. And the message, which is always fugitive, hides beneath a flexible technique.

In certain cases, Tawney invents her own technique. Take, for example, her half-concealing, curiously revealing flow of fibers over painted canvases or her mesmerizing *Clouds* in shimmering flux or her postcards elevated to a new form of communication. An inveterate traveler, she keeps in touch with her friends through picture postcards altered by various devices, including collage, watercolor, pastel, line drawing, and even such objects as feathers or photographs. These transformations, often assisted by the artist's own weblike calligraphy, require patient deciphering. Although at times the cards refer obliquely to the locale from which they originated, they go beyond the explicit and the topical. As in all Tawney's work, the past confronts the present, the East the West, the mundane the visionary; but more often it is the visionary that predominates.

Above all, however, it is her woven work that sets her apart as an innovator and a pioneer. Sometime around the middle of this century, she began experimenting with a new kind of what was then called weaving but now is better known as fiber work. Never forcing her material to perform counter to its fluid nature, she produced hangings that vary from intimate fragility to majestic power. Areas of transparency often permeate more solidly woven sections, thus allowing light to act both as a visual and symbolic force. Meaning is always what counts. Repeatedly, an ambiguous union of the tangible and the fleeting extends Tawney's work beyond familiar boundaries. Borrowing occasionally from American Indian woven baskets, with their intricate play of textures, and from a Far Eastern emphasis on the metaphysical and the mandala, she quietly developed a new vocabulary for fiber, a new freedom from conventional weaving techniques. It is no exaggeration to claim her as very likely the earliest animating spirit behind modern fiber art. And invariably she uses the materials she works with, no matter how unorthodox, to create her own idiosyncratic vision.

Lenore Tawney in her Wooster Street studio, with *Dove,* 1974.

A Tribute to Lenore

PAUL J. SMITH

White silence

   peace

a silk thread
      a feather
         a stone

a quiet line
      a splash of blue
black paper torn

      a written word

inner soul
      reflected

      a gift to the universe

The innovative and prolific output of Lenore Tawney has claimed her a significant place in the development of American art since World War II. This retrospective collection of work, assembled by the American Craft Museum, honors the imagination of an artist who has merged the past with the present and developed a body of work with a new aesthetic, one that has been an important influence in fiber both here and abroad.

In her life, Lenore has been a pioneer. During the 1950s, she was one of a few artists who began to explore fresh approaches to craft media. After first learning traditional weaving techniques, Lenore embarked on a private path of experimentation, pushing fiber to an unprecedented dimension. Along with such artists as ceramist Peter Voulkos, she created a new aesthetic for work in craft media that paralleled the abstract expressionist movement of the time. Her weavings, based on traditional tapestry techniques, soon evolved as drawings in thread with colorful and fanciful expressionist messages.

In the early 1960s, Lenore experimented with form to develop sculptural shapes. A series of sculptural weavings, which sparked a new direction in fiber art, soon had a major influence both in America and Europe. Her dynamic work inspired the pivotal 1963 exhibition "Woven Forms," which I organized at the Museum of Contemporary Crafts (now the American Craft Museum). Her subsequent works in fiber focused on a series of thematic subjects—the cross, the flag, the cloud. Like her earlier work, each represented an in-depth exploration and a new horizon of personal expression.

While Lenore is best known for the vast range of her fiber pieces, her collage works also have stature. The scope of subject matter contained in her assem-

blages is impressive. Each is made from an assortment of found objects that have been transformed into personalized icons. With paper, thread, a written word, or through found objects such as a feather or a pebble, she has created visual poetry. Each work transmits a quiet power that comes from her inner spirit, strength, and sensitivity. In many of the small collage pieces, one also can see the birth of ideas later developed in larger works.

I first met Lenore in 1957 when I came to New York to join the American Craft Council. She had just moved to New York from Chicago, to a studio at Coenties Slip, which was developing as a small colony of artists that included Robert Indiana and Agnes Martin. Through the years, Lenore has become a special friend. I remember visiting her lofts many times and viewing the environments she created. Each was a collage of art in process, with objects and materials all sensitively placed. Each space became a meditative setting reflecting her spiritual beliefs. Her current all-white loft has been transformed into an altar of objects and work, a cerebral space where one experiences peace, tranquility, and a presence of the unknown.

Lenore Tawney has followed a unique path as an artist. Her life, her environments, her spiritual pursuits, her love of nature and material, and her devotion to detail and craftsmanship are reflected in the more than one hundred works represented in this exhibition. Each is a poetic statement, whether it be a large cloud of threads suspended from above or a quail egg given an honored place on earth. Transformed by Lenore's personal vision, each has a ceremonial presence to share with the viewer.

Photographs of Lenore Tawney and her studio, by Paul J. Smith, 1985.

15

Messages from a Journey

KATHLEEN NUGENT MANGAN

Lenore Tawney has long been acknowledged as a pioneer in the transformation of contemporary fiber art. Her innovational contributions of the 1950s and 1960s paved the way for the revolution in fiber that was to come. Tawney's weavings broke away from the rectangle and the wall, hung freely in space, and assumed sculptural dimensions. Ultimately achieving architectural scale and monumental impact, her works in fiber were always characterized by passionate attention to detail and consummate craftsmanship.

Since the mid-1960s, Tawney's oeuvre has also included collage and assemblage. Intensely personal and intimate in scale, these works nonetheless reflect many of the same concerns evident in the weavings. Tawney's poetic sensitivity to materials is nowhere more apparent than here. And throughout the body of her work, a theme is stated; variations abound.

From the outset, Tawney's works were exhibited and collected internationally. Yet, despite the critical acclaim she has received, Tawney remains underrecognized. Hers is a private world, and its details have been closely guarded. She is elusive, enigmatic.

With this retrospective exhibition of Lenore Tawney's fiber, collage, and assemblage, the American

Craft Museum both honors her and reaffirms the significance of her contribution. It is the purpose of this catalogue to establish an accurate chronology of Tawney's life and work, to consider its impact, and to convey, through entries from her private journals and illustrations of the works themselves, the remarkable spirit of this American pioneer.

Beginnings

Leonora Agnes Gallagher was born in Lorain, Ohio, on May 10, 1907. One of five children of an Irish mother and Irish-American father, she was raised along the shores of Lake Erie and educated in a parochial school. The color blue, a spiritual color, tints the memories of her childhood—the blue of the water and the sky.

In 1927, Tawney left Lorain for Chicago, where one of her brothers had already settled. She found employment as a proofreader for a publisher of court opinions, eventually becoming head of her department. In the evenings, Tawney attended classes at the Art Institute of Chicago. It was in Chicago, through friends, that she met her future husband George Tawney, a young psychologist. Theirs was a happy yet tragically brief marriage. Following a sud-

Tawney and her cat, Pansy, Beekman Street studio, 1966.

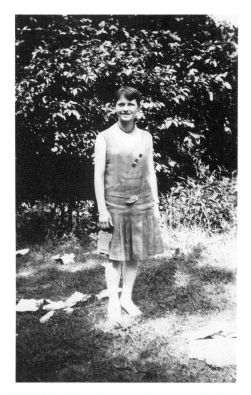

den illness, George Tawney died in 1943, a year and a half after their wedding.

Devastated and grieving deeply, Tawney moved to Urbana to be with her husband's family. There, she enrolled at the University of Illinois to study art. But Tawney was restless; in 1945, she traveled to Mexico for six months, and then returned to Chicago.

In 1946, she enrolled in the basic course at the Institute of Design, which had opened its doors in 1937 under the direction of Laszlo Moholy-Nagy. The program included studies in sculpture with Alexander Archipenko, drawing with Moholy-Nagy, drawing and watercolor painting with Emerson Woelffer, and weaving with Marli Ehrman. Tawney, a promising sculpture student, was invited by Archipenko for further studies at his studio in Woodstock, New York. With Archipenko, Tawney worked in clay, creating abstract, figurative forms. The work was constant and intense, requiring all her energy. After returning to Chicago, she faced a decision. To continue to work as she had in Woodstock demanded complete commitment, and Tawney was not yet ready to devote herself entirely to her work. She abandoned sculpture and destroyed much of her work.

Sometime after this, Tawney purchased a second-hand loom and began to weave. Even her earliest works—placemats and other functional pieces—found acceptance in juried exhibitions.[1] But a period of travel intervened. Tawney left for Europe in 1949, living in Paris for the next year and a half, and traveling extensively throughout Europe and North Africa.

Turning Point: Penland, 1954

The turning point in her work came in 1954 when she learned that Martta Taipale, the distinguished Finnish weaver, was to teach tapestry design at the Penland School of Crafts. Tawney went to North Carolina to study with Taipale. She later described the experience:

TOP: Tawney as a teenager, Lorain, Ohio.

BOTTOM: Three untitled sculptures, ca. 1947–48, fired clay, left to right: $13'' \times 7'' \times 3\frac{1}{2}''$; $9\frac{3}{4}'' \times 8\frac{1}{2}'' \times 4\frac{1}{2}''$; $13\frac{3}{4}'' \times 4'' \times 2''$. Collection Mrs. Jack Weinberg.

I was with her six weeks, and wove two tapestries of her design under her direction. The second one took five weeks of intensive eight-hour days. On the second half, I began to venture to mix my own colors. When I cut it off, I couldn't look at it; I hid it for half a day, then took it to Martta's studio and we looked at it together. Martta [was] a warm and wonderful person and an inspiring teacher. She said, "Color is like music," and I could see color soaring like Gothic arches in the sky.

I brought home what was left of my warp, attached it to my loom, made the sketch for *St. Francis and the Birds,* and began to weave my first tapestry alone. I was going to do it in dun colors, but it didn't turn out that way. The red and yellow and pink crept in; the purple sidled up.[2]

Tawney's sketch for *St. Francis* was in black and white, as were sketches for her subsequent tapestries. The color and structure of the works developed spontaneously on the loom.

Tawney at the loom, Penland School of Crafts, North Carolina, 1954.

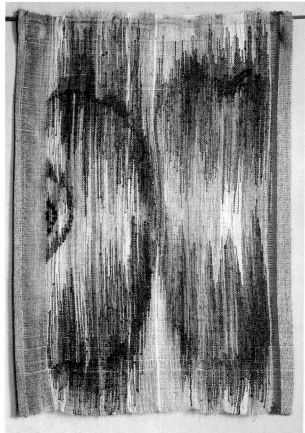

TOP: Tawney in her Chicago studio, 1957.

BOTTOM: *Two Apples*, 1957, silk, wool, 24″ × 18″.
Commissioned by Marshall Field, Chicago.

Weavings of the 1950s

Tawney no longer resisted complete devotion to work. She worked steadily and experimented, breaking the traditional rules of weaving when she found them restrictive. In 1955, she began the open-warp weavings that brought her both acclaim and criticism. These controversial pieces juxtaposed areas of plain weave and/or laid-in designs with large areas of unwoven warp. They were hung away from the wall, maximizing the contrast of opacity and transparency and the impact of light and shadow. The works were characterized by rich combinations of materials—linens, wools, and silks of various weights and textures; as early as 1955, they incorporated feathers.

Tawney was offered one of her first commissions in 1957—a tapestry for a new restaurant opened by Marshall Field. The unusual circumstances of the commission were significant, revealing Tawney's fiercely independent spirit and indicating the way she would always work. Tawney did not submit a design, but worked freely on her own. In this case, she wove two tapestries: one as close as possible to what she believed the client wanted; the other, to satisfy herself. Marshall Field took both pieces.

At the time, Tawney discussed her feelings about commissioned work:

> I want to please the customer, naturally, but I must first please myself. To free myself to do what I want with the work, I must throw off the desire to please, then do what I want and plan to keep it if the customer doesn't like it. . . . Most of the time, I simply work on my own ideas. I work all the time.[3]

In a 1957 article on Tawney for *Craft Horizons*, the painter Margo Hoff noted, ''Her work is controversial, but the great response to it indicates that there is a kind of revolt going on in the United States against craftsmanship dictated by traditional methods and the limits of the tool.''[4] Hoff was correct: These early works were the beginning of a revolution in fiber.

In November 1957, Tawney left Chicago for New York and a studio at 27 Coenties Slip.[5] In this vital community of artists, Jack Youngerman was her

landlord and Agnes Martin her close friend and neighbor. Years later, Tawney recalled the move in a journal entry: "It [the Coenties Slip loft] needed everything—painting, heating, but first, cleaning out. I had sent only a very small bed, refrigerator, loom, and threads. I drove my Daimler from Chicago with my cat, Pansy."[6]

Another journal entry: "I left Chicago," she reflected, "to seek a barer life, closer to reality, without all the *things* that clutter and fill our lives. . . . The truest thing in my life was my work. I wanted my life to be as true. [I] almost gave up my life for my work, seeking a life of the spirit."[7]

After eight months at Coenties Slip, Tawney

TOP: Tawney in her Daimler, Coenties Slip, New York, 1958.

BOTTOM: Tawney in her Coenties Slip studio, 1958.

moved around the corner to 27 South Street, where she leased three floors of a former sailmaker's loft, with a cathedral ceiling on the top floor. Here, with soaring space and a magnificent view of the East River, she set up her studio. Tawney worked incessantly, creating tapestries of tremendous scale, experimenting, and exploring new ideas. "The idea of weaving in volume floated up to consciousness this morning," she wrote in June 1958, "as I awoke nervous and excited all day thinking about it."[8]

The Interchurch Center Commission

At this time, Tawney was offered an important commission: a tapestry for the narthex of the chapel of the Interchurch Center, on Riverside Drive. She accepted, under the same conditions that she had earlier established with Marshall Field. The chapel architect, Frederick Dunn, explained in a letter to his client: "Miss Tawney does not make preliminary sketches, but instead works direct. She proposed to discuss subject matter and weave a tapestry for the narthex, which the building committee is not obligated to accept if the members do not wish to have it."[9] Tawney's unorthodox proposal was accepted, and she began work on the ten-and-one-half-by-twelve-and-one-half-foot *Nativity in Nature* in 1959.

The tapestry, woven in three sections joined together, was completed in 1960 and installed for the review of the building committee in May. Tawney's *Nativity* depicted the Virgin and Child in a landscape. However, the Virgin appeared only in outline, and her Child was represented simply as pure light. Owls, a heron, and other water birds surrounded the Mother and Child amidst rich foliage. The members of the committee were disconcerted. The *Nativity* was too abstract, too much in need of interpretation. After great discussion, the piece was rejected.

Although the search for another weaver and a more traditional religious vision was initiated, Frederick Dunn remained supportive, convinced that Tawney's tapestry was the right piece for the narthex. He wrote to his client, emphasizing that the color and texture were perfect for the space, and

elaborating that "the tapestry . . . has all the dignity of a Byzantine mosaic, which dignity owes much to the simplified drafting of the figures." He continued, "The concept to me is most poetic in that the Christ Child is shown only as a blaze of light. In the Bible, John (1:4–9) speaks of Jesus as 'light.'"[10]

Dunn was persuasive. Not all the members of the building committee or the Center's board of trustees had seen the tapestry. He urged a second review, which Tawney permitted only with extreme reluctance. ("I said one rejection was enough," she later commented.)[11] This time the decision was favorable, and the acquisition of the tapestry was at last approved.

Transition/ The Staten Island Exhibition

All the while, Tawney carried on work in tapestry and open weave. She drew inspiration from nature (in particular, from a variety of birds), while simultaneously working on completely abstract compositions. She created innovative double-woven pieces,[12] and went on to weave the monumental *Triune* (nine by nine feet) in 1961. Fascinated by Peruvian textiles, Tawney studied gauze weave with Lili Blumenau in the same year, and began to experiment with gauze-weave techniques in transitional pieces.

Nineteen sixty-one was also the year of another important event—Tawney's first major solo exhibition, at the Staten Island Museum.[13] Curator James Coggin recalls visiting her loft on South Street and being struck by the vitality of the work and the radical departure in fiber that it represented. Forty works woven over a six-year period were selected for the exhibition. In a brief statement for the exhibition catalogue, Agnes Martin focused on the originality of Tawney's vision:

To see new and original expression in a very old medium, and not just one new form but a complete new form in each piece of work, is wholly unlooked for, and is a wonderful and gratifying experience.

With directness and clarity, with what appears to be complete certainty of image, beyond primitive determi-

Nativity in Nature, 1960, linen, wool, silk, 126" × 150". The Interchurch Center, New York.

TO THE GLORY OF GOD AND THE SERVICE OF MANKIND THIS CHAPEL IS DEDICATED IN LOVING MEMORY OF
CHARLES ULRICK BAY · AMERICAN AMBASSADOR TO NORWAY 1946–1953 · AND AS A TRIBUTE TO
DR· & MRS· NORMAN VINCENT PEALE BY THE CHARLES ULRICK & JOSEPHINE BAY FOUNDATION

nation or any other aggressiveness, sensitive and accurate down to the last thread, this work flows out without hesitation and with a consistent quality.[14]

Reviews revealed the excitement about the exhibition. Writing for *Craft Horizons*, Alice Adams described Tawney's "enormous range of technique and . . . rare sense of image and object as one. The hangings . . . are remarkable for the consistently free and courageous approach to the materials used." New directions were certainly indicated. "The more recent works often burst the confines of warp and weft, by use of gauze constructions, by carrying a distorted warp to its furthest conclusions."[15]

Woven Forms

Experimentation continued. Tawney had ordered a large quantity of linen in black and natural, although she was uncertain as to how it would be used. Some of the yarn was made especially heavy, to her order. She stripped her work of its luxuriant color, proceeding in black and natural, and invented an open reed that allowed her to change the shape of the works as she wove them.

Now the contours of the works could go in and out, "constructed," in Tawney's words, "as expanding, contracting, aspiring forms—sometimes expanding at the edges while contracting in the center."[16] Tawney worked continuously and intuitively on these new pieces. "I put on a certain length of warp and wove to the end of it," she said, "something in me knowing what I was doing."[17] Only a small section at a time was visible as she worked on the loom, but the work flowed out in tall and elegant forms. New sources of inspiration were apparent: knots recalled the huge knots on the tugboats she watched from her riverfront studio as well as those on the garment carts along Seventh Avenue. Braids reflected her fascination with ancient Egyptian headdresses and wigs. "This new work," she wrote in 1962, "is called *Woven Forms*. It is sculptural."[18]

With these works, Tawney transformed woven surface into expressive three-dimensional form. Like her earlier weavings, the new works hung freely in space, but now they went further to exploit areas of solid and void, and through their irregular shapes, they achieved strong sculptural presence. Some of the works incorporated primitive artifacts that Tawney had collected; others were embellished with feathers.

Agnes Martin named the new pieces *The King, The Queen, The Bride,* and so on, and in 1963 they were exhibited in the seminal "Woven Forms," at the Museum of Contemporary Crafts (now the American Craft Museum). Tawney's name for her new body of work was used as the exhibition's title, and she contributed twenty-two of the forty-three pieces on display. Four other American weavers—Alice Adams, Sheila Hicks, Dorian Zachai, and Claire Zeisler—were also represented with innovative works. "Woven Forms" thus chronicled the climate of experimentation in fiber that characterized the period. It was the first major exhibition of this vital, highly original direction, and its impact was enormous.[19]

In his introduction to the catalogue, curator Paul J. Smith discussed the exhibition's "sculptural shapes of interlaced threads." "In these hangings," Smith stated, "not only the created surface but the created shape becomes an expressive formal ele-

OPPOSITE: *Triune,* 1961, linen, wook, silk, 109$\frac{1}{2}$″ × 104″. Collection The Metropolitan Museum of Art, New York, Purchase the Louis Comfort Tiffany Foundation Gift, 1983.

LEFT: *Dark River,* 1962, linen, wood, 163″ × 22$\frac{1}{2}$″, in South Street studio. Collection The Museum of Modern Art, New York, Greta Daniel Design Fund.

BELOW: *Dark River* (detail).

ment. This is the result of a reevaluation of the weaving process as implemental in varying the shape of the finished object. . . . Form is determined by distortion of the set pattern of the warp and weft while the piece is still on the loom. Thus, the artist's search for form is reflected in the finished hanging."[20]

The Solel Commission

Tawney received another major commission in 1963, this time for the veil covering the ark at Congregation Solel's new temple in Highland Park, Illinois. Just as surely as *Nativity in Nature* had reflected

her work of the late 1950s, the ark veil was created in the spirit of the woven forms. In form and color, the veil was pure, woven in natural linen, embellished with braids and knots wrapped in twenty-four karat gold wire. Tawney's thoughts on the piece were recorded in the Solel newsletter:

This curtain is a veil of light and dark that hangs between you and the mystery of the Holy Scrolls—not hiding but enhancing the mystery.

The light at the edges is a continuation of the design of the veil, giving to the veil a feeling as of trembling in light and space, an atmosphere of lightness, in the sense both of weight and of light. There has never been an ark veil like this one. It was conceived out of the place of Solel. Give it the honor of seeing it as it is, *in itself,* rather than judging it by comparison with the old.

It stands wrapped in dignity and silence, protecting the sacred doctrine, commanding solemn joyousness.[21]

Other New Directions of the 1960s

The following year, during the First World Congress of Craftsmen, sponsored by the American Craftsmen's Council, in New York, Tawney visited a New Jersey factory to observe a Jacquard loom. Excited and inspired by the loom's trembling threads, she looked up old Jacquard weavings and patterns at the Cooper Union and studied the loom for a year at the Textile Institute, in Philadelphia. Out of this experience came a series of drawings in ink on graph paper, systematic and precise, each drawing, each fine line a meditation.[22]

Concurrently, Tawney began to work in collage and assemblage. Objects gathered over the years—pages of rare books, eggs, feathers, pebbles, the skeletons of birds—were infused with new meaning and purpose. The faded pages and bleached skeletons of these intimate works testified to the passage of time; the text elements that they incorporated were no longer legible, yet they possessed a heightened power to communicate mysterious, elusive messages. While Tawney's weavings had boldly announced new directions, these new works whispered their quiet, mystical secrets.

The highly personal postcard collages that Tawney sent to friends developed at the same time. Born of the desire to communicate without sending specific messages, they were cryptic notations, often enriched by Tawney's fine handwriting. They were signs, she says, thrown to the winds.

Tawney continued to work on the woven forms, but simultaneously began a series of small, densely woven shields (as she called them), squares, crosses, and masks. Reflective of her deep response to primitive art, these fetishlike weavings were made with thousands of threads, tiny feathers, and pre-Columbian shells and beads. And, like the drawings inspired by the Jacquard loom, the infinite time involved in their creation represented a meditation.

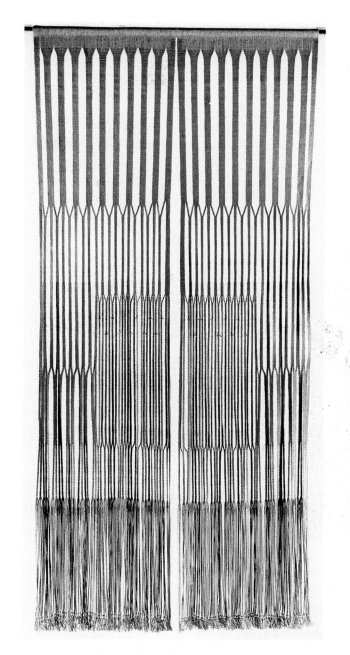

OPPOSITE: Installation of weavings by Lenore Tawney in "Woven Forms," Museum of Contemporary Crafts (now American Craft Museum), New York, 1963.

ABOVE: Ark veil, 1963, linen, gold wire, 120" × 54". Congregation Solel, Highland Park, Illinois.

Synthesis: Weavings of the 1970s

As the work developed, Tawney recalls wondering whether the collage and fiber would ever come together. The solution came from within (as had the major breakthroughs of her earlier work) in 1974. Collage and woven structure combined in a series of works based upon the image of the circle within the square. In these pieces, the collage was made as the works were woven, and a new synthesis was achieved.

Tawney's forms were now distilled into basic, powerful universal symbols: the cross (representing the meeting of opposites and the point at which linear and eternal time meet), and the repeated image of the circle within the square (a symbol of unity). While some of the works were woven in bright, saturated hues, black and natural became dominant again, and once more the weavings (now seven-feet and nine-feet square), achieved strong architectural presence.

In 1974, Tawney also created a series of weavings and collages based upon the image of the flag.

> For years, I had thought of flags and banners. So I finally did it . . . [After the political events of the last several years,] I felt our flag was being shamed, hence it is "untitled." It goes back to beginnings. Instead of Betsy Ross's petticoat, a friend gave me her bluejeans, and the bluejeans buttons are the stars, dark and not proud. But still the sentiments of that early time are there, the "true-blue," the good and strong linen.[23]

In 1976, continuing to explore the compositional format of the circle within the square, Tawney created the monumental collage-weaving *Waters above the Firmament* (twelve by twelve feet). It would be her last work on the loom. Again, Tawney was on the threshold of change and an important new body of work.

TOP: Tawney in her Spring Street studio, ca. 1967.

BOTTOM: *Mask with Horsehair*, ca. 1967, linen, horsehair, gold, pre-Columbian beads, 24" × 8". Collection The Art Institute of Chicago, Restricted gift of Mrs. Tiffany Blake in honor of Mrs. John V. Farwell III.

Waters above the Firmament, Wooster Street studio, 1976.

The General Services Administration Commission

While traveling in India in early 1977, Tawney received a letter from the General Services Administration inviting her to create a commissioned piece for the lobby of the new Federal Building in Santa Rosa, California. After returning to the United States, she flew to California to visit the site with Donald Thalacker, the director of G.S.A.'s Art-in-Architecture program.

As Tawney recalled the visit:

> The lobby was one hundred and sixty feet long, twenty-five feet high, and the outside wall was glass. This space was divided imperceptibly into four sections of forty feet.
>
> We walked up and down and around. Don spoke of a "ceiling piece." I could not see anything I had done hanging in this space. But I . . . knew that if I waited,

without impatience, an inspiration would arise out of silence. I chose one of the forty-foot spaces.[24]

Tawney accepted the commission, which accorded her complete artistic freedom. Inspiration arose in response to a major drought hitting California at the time, and she conceived the idea of a cloud. A rectangular canvas, thirty feet long by five feet wide, was painted blue, and from it linen threads (more than 2,550 of them, in three shades of blue) were suspended from a grid pattern in sixteen-foot lengths. The creation of the piece was again a meditation, for each of these threads had to be carefully measured, counted, knotted, rolled up, and finally rolled down. Due to the size of the piece, it was impossible to see it completed until it was installed in California. *Cloud Series IV* was dedicated in May 1978, and although a certain degree of controversy ensued, it was clear that once more Tawney had expanded the expressive potential of fiber.

ABOVE: Tawney spreading the painted canvas of *Cloud Series IV* in a field to dry, 1977.

OPPOSITE: *Cloud Series IV*, 1978, canvas, linen, 16' × 30' × 5'. Santa Rosa Federal Building, Santa Rosa, California.

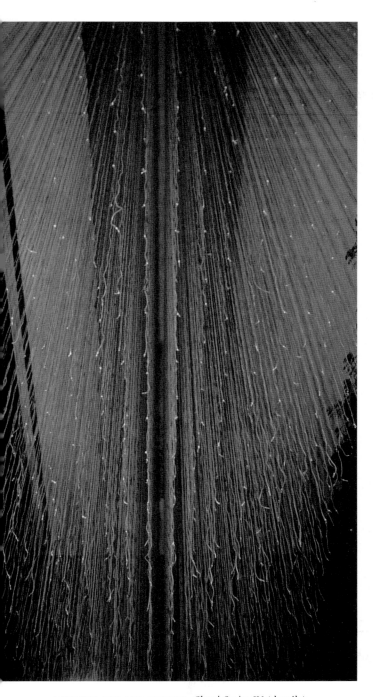

OPPOSITE, TOP AND BOTTOM: *Cloud Series IV* (details).

LEFT: *Cloud Series IV* (detail).

RIGHT: *Cloud Series IV* seen from beneath.

Cloud Sculptures and
Other Works of the 1980s

Two other major commissions for cloud sculptures in public spaces followed. In 1981, Tawney installed *Cloud Series VI* in the Frank J. Lausche State Office Building, in Cleveland, Ohio, and in 1983, she was commissioned by the State of Connecticut for a piece in the library of Western Connecticut State University, in Danbury.

As the cloud series developed, other work progressed. In 1985, she created a series of collage chairs, rendered as unsittable as the pages of rare books had become unreadable twenty years before. In defiance of gravity, the chairs took wing: They hung from the ceiling, divorced from context and function.

Today, Tawney's cloud sculptures and her work in collage and assemblage are ongoing. A quiet but insistent sense of purpose and an ethereal unity are evident throughout. She continues to experiment in new works—searching, refining, and ultimately revealing glimpses of a singular and poetic inner landscape.

I AM ESPECIALLY INDEBTED to Lenore Tawney for her assistance throughout the preparation of this exhibition. She has generously shared a great deal of heretofore unpublished material with me, and for her patience and cooperation I am extremely grateful.

The editor has taken the opportunity to correct inaccuracies in previously published material.
K.N.M.

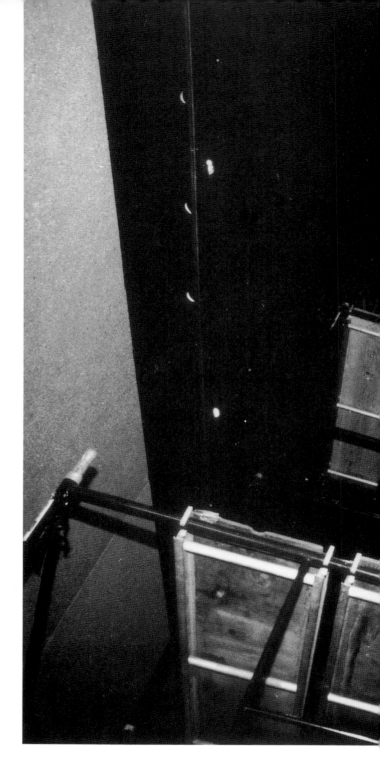

ABOVE: Tawney installing *Cloud Series VI*, 1981, canvas, linen, 16' × 32' × 8'. Frank J. Lausche State Office Building, Cleveland, Ohio.

RIGHT: Tawney installing *Cloud Series VII*, 1983, Western Connecticut State University, Danbury.

NOTES

1. Tawney's work was included in the "International Textile Exhibition," at the University of North Carolina, in 1949 (for which Anni Albers had been a member of the jury), and "Good Design," an exhibition of home furnishings selected by the Museum of Modern Art, New York, for the Merchandise Mart, Chicago, January 1950.

2. Margo Hoff, "Lenore Tawney: The Warp Is Her Canvas," *Craft Horizons* 17 (November/December 1957): 16.

3. Ibid., 19.

4. Ibid., 15.

5. This was the first of Tawney's eight loft residences in New York. None of these had been residential, and each living space required building from scratch. Many of the buildings were demolished, necessitating the frequent moves that repeatedly disrupted Tawney's work.

6. Lenore Tawney, journal entry, 1987.

7. Tawney, journal entry, December 4, 1967.

8. Tawney, journal entry, June 4, 1958. Tawney originally envisioned multiple layers of open-warp weave (up to five), woven one behind the other. Each of these different but related layers was to be separated by space at the top to achieve depth and dimension. The idea was never fully realized (although several double-woven works did follow), but the concept is significant, revealing Tawney's search for three-dimensional form.

9. Frederick Dunn to the Interchurch Center, November 24, 1958.

10. Dunn to Charles Van Anden, Interchurch Center, August 31, 1960.

11. Tawney, in conversation, September, 1989.

12. In a letter dated December 3, 1959, Tawney described these to her friend and Chicago dealer, Marna Johnson. "[One piece is] double-woven, that is, two pieces woven at the same time on the same warp, woven together at the top but separated all the way down from there. It should be hung . . . to separate the two sides, so that there is space inside as well as behind."

13. Mildred Constantine and Jack Lenor Larsen celebrate this as the first major exhibit of American art fabrics, "the point at which the art fabric was healthfully and joyously launched in America." See *Beyond Craft: The Art Fabric* (New York: Van Nostrand, Reinhold 1972), 45.

14. Agnes Martin, *Lenore Tawney,* Staten Island Museum, New York, November 19, 1961–January 7, 1962.

15. Alice Adams, "Lenore Tawney," *Craft Horizons* 22 (January/February 1962): 39.

16. Ann Wilson, *Woven Forms,* Museum of Contemporary Crafts (now American Craft Museum), New York, March 22–May 12, 1963.

17. Tawney, in conversation, September, 1989.

18. Tawney to Marna Johnson, August 1, 1962.

19. This climate of experimentation is discussed by Erika Billeter in her essay in this catalogue. As Billeter notes, in "Woven Forms," Tawney took "the concept of a new textile art to the extreme," but her experiments were not isolated. The exploration of new directions in fiber was an international concern during the 1960s.

20. Paul J. Smith, *Woven Forms.*

21. *The Pathfinder* (newsletter of Congregation Solel), September 17, 1964.

22. A later series of constructions also grew out of the Jacquard experience.

23. Textile Arts Club 1975–76 program, Cleveland Museum of Art.

24. Donald W. Thalacker, *The Place of Art in the World of Architecture* (New York: Chelsea House Publishers, 1980), 162.

LEFT: Tawney installing *Cloud Series VI,* 1981.

A Very Personal
Word for L. T.

ERIKA   BILLETER

I met Lenore Tawney in 1964. As a young curator, I took my first, rather daring step into the world of exhibitions with a group show presenting Lenore Tawney, Claire Zeisler, and Sheila Hicks. Today, I realize this was a genuine avant-garde event. The new form of tapestry was being shown in Europe for the first time—before the Lausanne Biennale, where, shortly after our exhibition, innovative directions in the art were acknowledged. In this initial exhibition, Lenore Tawney was the one artist who had taken the concept of a new textile art to the extreme. The reviews, though, were in keeping with the tenor of the times; no one understood the transparent weavings that defined space with a delicate network of threads.

I entered the avant-garde with Lenore, and to this day, twenty-five years later, I have never lost track of her or her work. On two further occasions, I had the pleasure of showing her in large-scale exhibitions: the important and ground-breaking "Weich und Plastisch: Soft-Art," at the Kunsthaus Zurich, in 1979, and before that at the Lausanne Biennale, in 1975. Working with Lenore has always been special. Her work is born from meditation—the source of her creativity. Who else could carefully tie, one by one, thousands of threads to make a cloud? In Zurich,

Lenore Tawney installing cloud sculpture, "Weich und Plastisch: Soft-Art," Kunsthaus Zurich, 1979.

we watched, spellbound, the creation of this work, observing her as she sat enthroned on her high seat. At the time, she sent me a postcard every day, insisting, although subtlely, that she needed more space for her cloud. Each of these cards is a work of art. In fact, everything she touches is transformed into art. Her collection of the seemingly unnecessary, forgotten, or overlooked—the eggs, feathers, and shells that crowd her drawers, closets, her entire living space—have but one purpose: to be transformed into art. At some point, Lenore will pick up an object—after having stored it subconsciously in her mind for a long time—and start to work with it. She makes collages from pages of old books and found objects. With her incredibly beautiful calligraphy, she writes on sky-blue-tinted paper, collages a small item onto it, and thereby creates a highly sensitive piece of art that is imbued with her personality. When you own a work by Lenore, you possess a piece of her soul; it renders the work alive.

Lenore once said that her first woven forms had already existed inside her. She worked as if in a trance to bring forth all those wonderful creations: *Lekythos, The King,* and *The Queen.* This process applies not only to her weavings but to her entire output. Lenore works—whether at weavings or col-

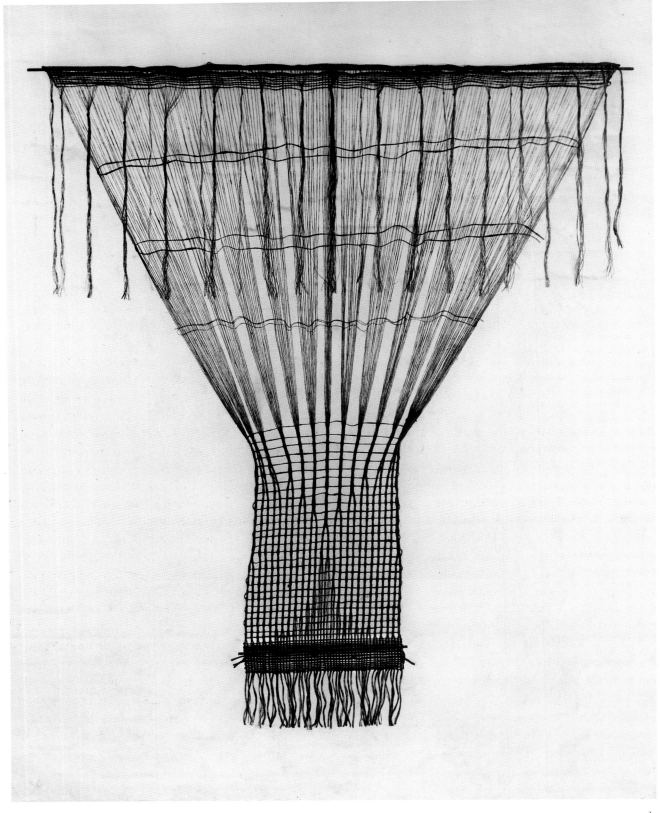

Lekythos, 1963, linen, 50″ × 31¾″.

lages—from a world within, which is what makes the result so extraordinary. She has followed her own path, without paying attention to trends. Ironically, her work appears both timeless and contemporary, and actually expresses the trends of the 1960s. These are works that changed the face of textile art; they have no precursors. To see them in a greater context, we must turn back to history, to Peruvian gauze weavings. These textiles inspired Lenore, and she describes the impact the techniques had on her woven forms:

> They were done in the Peruvian gauze-weave technique, where the threads are crossed over all the way across the loom. You do this by hand. Then you return and they all jump back to where they were. Then you go across and cross every one again—on a stick, you know—and then back again, and so forth. With the new reed, I could make the weaving go out and in.*

To revitalize textile art or, more precisely, tapestry was a means of expressing the zeitgeist of the early 1960s. Female Polish artists, led by Magdalena Abakanowicz, began to discover new textile materials and forms. In Yugoslavia, Jagoda Buic was another female artist who changed the traditional idea of tapestry. In the United States, Lenore Tawney, Claire Zeisler, and Sheila Hicks were in the vanguard of this movement, which, because of their work, took a completely new direction. Although a part of this new wave, Tawney still followed her own path. This independence may have been due to the sculptor Archipenko, who introduced her to the concept of sculptural forms in different materials. Her weavings continue to draw from a formal simplicity and sincerity that is wed to the lightness, the fragility of the material. Each work has a sculptural quality. But she also seeks effects that are foreign to sculptural forms. *Lekythos* (1962) is made from free-hanging warp threads; a fountain, as Lenore sees it. Everything flows and evokes a sense of flowing. Fifteen years later, she profited from these experiences when she created her clouds.

*This quote and the others that appear are taken from *Lenore Tawney: A Personal World* (Brookfield, Connecticut: Brookfield Craft Center, 1978).

From the time of her early work, the categories of "fine art" and "applied art," or "craft," were strictly separated. Yet, Lenore's work stands somewhere between the two. This very independence moved her ultimately into the category of fine arts. In 1964, she had already completed a series of drawings inspired by the Jacquard loom. These drawings have nothing in common with applied art, or craft. They are free interpretations. "Every line is made with my mind being right with the line," she has said. And on another occasion: "I kept making these drawings for the whole year. They were like a meditation, each drawing, each line. They were wonderful to do. All done on graph paper, except for some later ones." In these drawings, she alternated between weaving a line and drawing a line, until, suddenly, they became congruent. Her thoughts circled around the thread as the material of an art form.

To classify Lenore does her an injustice. She has always been more than a textile artist. Even though she worked with thread as her medium, she was a free spirit. While still devoted to her new woven forms and drawings, she also developed collages and assemblages that for many years were to be her main occupation. She created boxes—secret-bearing containers in which miniature worlds of small, collected items are preserved. She discovered old books as work material. In the late 1960s, as if she had forgotten that her weavings had just started a revolution, she was busy working her found objects, collected over many years, into pieces of art. During that time she went to India, where her talents developed further. Meditation, an integral part of her life, from then on had an even greater significance. As for many of her countrymen—Mark Rothko, Sam Francis, Barnett Newman—Asia was the place she felt at home. It became her genius loci. Her collages and assemblages are like small altars of meditation, which distinguishes them from everything done before. With this new work, she stepped into a long-standing European art tradition that has its roots in folk-art inventions.

What Lenore has in common with this European tradition, though, is merely an art form; her objects trouvés have their own purpose. Kurt Schwitters glued together the leftover waste pieces of a culture; in her loft, Lenore carefully stores her found objects, which, in themselves, are things of beauty. Sometimes—as with her pigeon eggs—she adds a tender, soft tint of light blue. Everything becomes light, untouchable. She glues together old papers, writes on them, and paints across them with watercolors, working them in the most careful fashion so as not to diminish their fragility. Little chests and cupboards can be mystical and magical when they contain small bones. She loves certain objects in which she sees things that escape the normal eye. One discovery she made at a homeopath's office particularly inspired her. When the medicine cabinet was opened, ''I saw all these little bottles and they had little corks. I just lost my head again. I thought they were so wonderful.'' This visit resulted in a small collage of bottle corks on old collaged papers: *Epître* (1967).

It is this enthusiasm and rapture for the objects she transforms that make her collages unique. Although she stands amidst an art-historical tradition, she carries the tradition much further. The emotional involvement that drives her, and from which all her work stems, recalls Meret Oppenheim. Oppenheim's work is also embedded in tradition, and she, too, has set her own milestones.

Writing plays an important part in Lenore's work. Here, as well, existing traditions bear an influence. Since Picasso—and later, the dadaists and surrealists—calligraphy has become a potent means of composition in painting. Using old characters and her own handwriting, Lenore plays with existing printed writings. She designs postcards, which she then sends to friends as a means of communication in themselves rather than as part of a continuing verbal dialogue. For the most part, the texts are illegible, but the composition is made of Lenore's own writing. Writing within a picture, or a picture of writing, is an Asian formula for picture creations.

Her mental and emotional readiness to adopt Asian culture, yet not copy it, once again becomes apparent.

In certain works, the two forms of Lenore's creative expression have synthesized: She has combined weaving with collage. In one especially beautiful piece, *Waters above the Firmament* (1974), a circle is placed in a square—the perfect, eternal form—which brings to mind C. G. Jung, for whom circle and square represented the metaphor of the inner self. It is not by chance that these two forms keep recurring in Lenore's work. They are mantric signs that she found through her studies of Taoism. But she did not really have to discover them; to express the inner self has been her intention from the very beginning.

In 1977, Lenore embarked on a new creative journey. Her series of clouds, those environments of threads, came about, created through a work process in which she forgets time—has to forget time, in fact, because the work never seems to end. In Asia, she learned to live timelessly; it is part of her rhythm of life. "It is not patience," she says. "I'm not just patiently doing it, because I love to do it. It's done with devotion. It's just working."

When Claes Oldenburg installed his first soft props into environments in the 1960s, a new art form was created, which was used by artists with great success until the close of the last decade. In 1973, Colette created her legendary living room, "My Living Environment." Prior to that, in 1965, the Japanese artist Yayoi Kusama had created her "Endless Love Room," made from foam covered with cloth. And Alan Shields, as well, gave us his transparent spaces. Soft materials, especially textile materials, became important for the creation of artistic spaces that could be walked in and lived in. The *Cloud* series is a part of that era, but it is more of an art form than all the other environments of those years. This was a space we could walk through, defined by threads hanging down from above; but to walk through it was to disturb its closed beauty. The space is more a meditation room, from which, as with a shrine, one keeps a respectful distance.

Lenore's hands touched more than thirteen hundred linen threads, separately tying each one to a canvas base. To each thread she has given something of her self, so that her soul may be perceived by those able to sense it. For the others, her soul is hidden by thirteen hundred threads.

Installation of weavings by Lenore Tawney, "Gewebte Formen," Kunstgewerbemuseum Zurich, 1964.

Plates

OPPOSITE: *Bound Man* (detail), 1957, wool, silk, linen, goathair, 84″ × 36″. Collection American Craft Museum, New York.

ACCOMPANYING PLATES: Entries from private journals by Lenore Tawney, 1957–88.

OPPOSITE:
Untitled, ca. 1947–48
Fired clay
$13 \times 7 \times 3\frac{1}{2}$
Collection Mrs. Jack Weinberg

Untitled, ca. 1947–48
Fired clay
$13\frac{3}{4} \times 4 \times 2$
Collection Mrs. Jack Weinberg

Untitled, ca. 1947–48
Fired clay
$9\frac{3}{4} \times 8\frac{1}{2} \times 4\frac{1}{2}$
Collection Mrs. Jack Weinberg

The primordial
mystery of weaving &
spinning has been experi-
enced in projection upon the
Great Mother who weaves the
web of life & spins the thread of
fate, regardless of whether she appears as one
Great Spinstress or, as so frequently, in a lunar
triad.   It is not by accident that we speak
of the body's "tissues," for the tissue woven
by the Feminine in the cosmos & in the
uterus of woman is life & destiny.
And astrology, the study of a destiny
governed by the stars, teaches that both
begin at once, at the temporal moment
of birth.

Thus the Great Goddesses are weavers,
in Egypt as in Greece, among the Germanic
peoples & the Mayans. And because "reality"
is wrought by the Great Weavers, all
such activities as plaiting, weaving &
knotting belong to the fate-governing
activity of the woman who, as Bachofen
discovered, is a spinner & weaver in her natural aspect.

St. Francis and the Birds,
1954
Wool
$32\frac{1}{2} \times 17\frac{1}{2}$

the warp was woven at noon
the woof in the house of dawn
the reel in the hall of the sun...

Wrought on the loom
Danced on the treads...

Golden gown woven for the moon
Shimmering veil for the little sun.

                    old Estonian song

= kneeling, Rilke thought, is the proper
posture for the artist. He must have
experienced the mystery of kneeling,
must know that a man upon his
knees "is greater, spiritually speaking,
than a man standing upright."
otherwise he risks forfeiting that
divine grace without which a
work of art remains empty.
the artist who kneels before his
work concentrates his feelings on
his heart.

Bound Man, 1957
Wool, silk, linen, goathair
84 × 36
Collection American Craft Museum
New York

Yellows, 1958
Wool, linen
$84 \times 50\frac{1}{2}$

Jupiter, 1959
Wool, silk
53×41
Collection American Craft Museum
New York
Gift of the Johnson Wax Company,
from Objects: USA

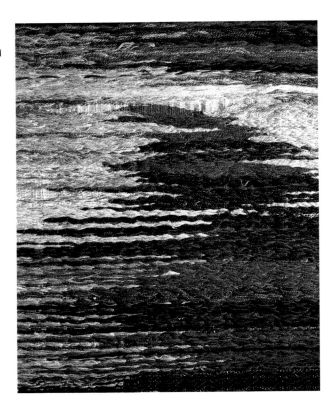

Detail of *Jupiter*, 1959

fine filaments like spiderweb spenaerel   5AM
        picture hanging in ctr as in space   5/19/57
                                              NYC

add fine silver thread here & there glint of rain
                                    sparks of early morning

explosion of crystals inner & outer
sharp cries of birds
cooing soft of doves

Lost and Proud, 1957
Linen, wool, silk
43 × 51$\frac{1}{2}$

Owls, ca. 1961
Linen, wool, graphite
$41 \times 10\frac{1}{2}$

small
hexagonals to
make Design

OPPOSITE, LEFT:
The Judge, 1961
Linen
124×14

OPPOSITE, RIGHT:
Vespers, 1961
Linen
82×21

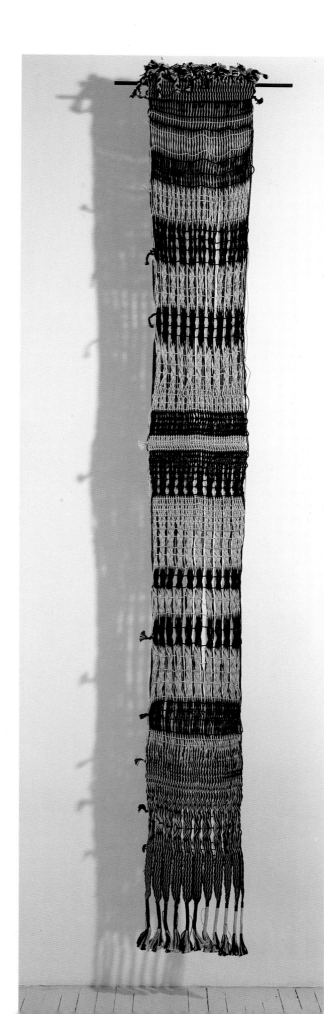
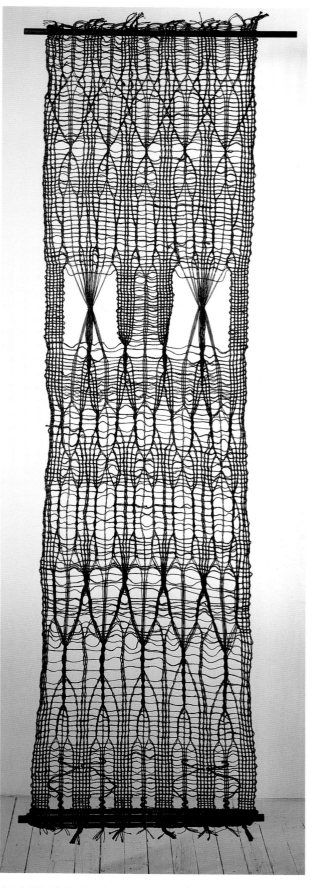

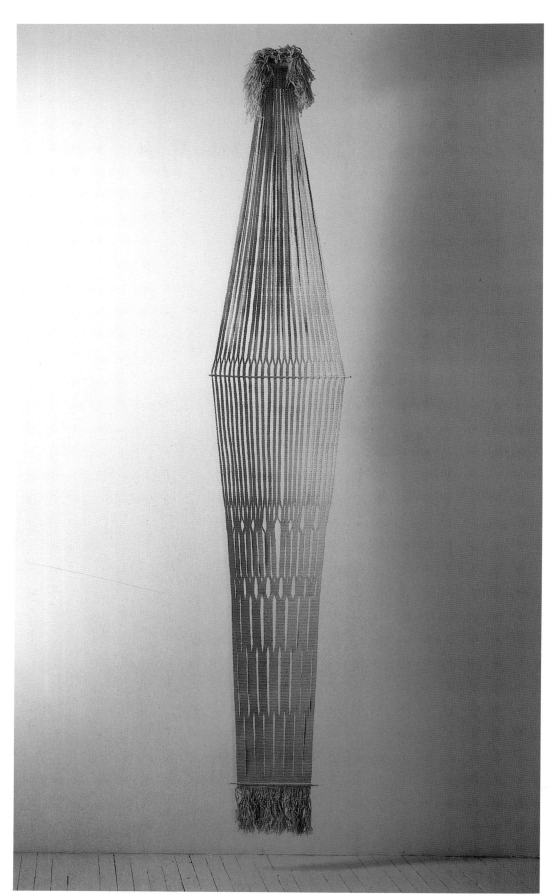

Orinoco, 1967
Linen
129 × 22½ × 4

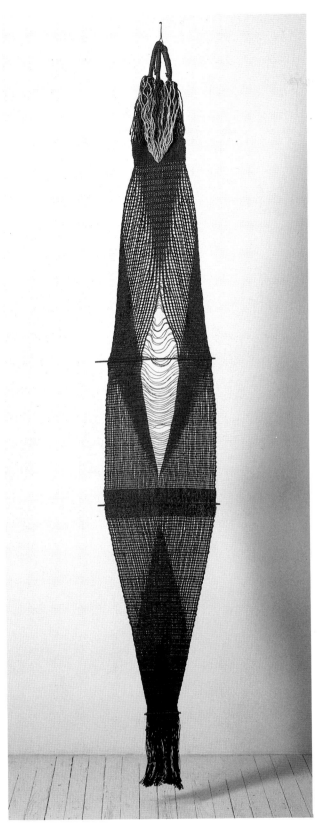

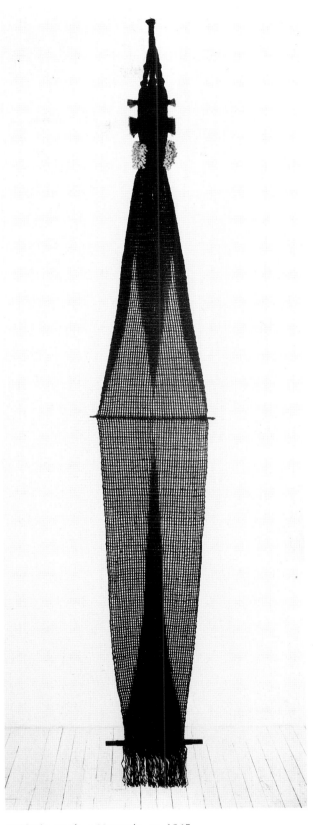

Black Woven Form (Fountain), 1966
Linen
103 × 15¼
Collection American Craft Museum, New York

Inside the Earth, a Mountain, ca. 1965
Linen
103 × 16½ × 2¾

The King I, 1962
Linen
148 × 31

The Queen, 1962
Linen
160 × 30

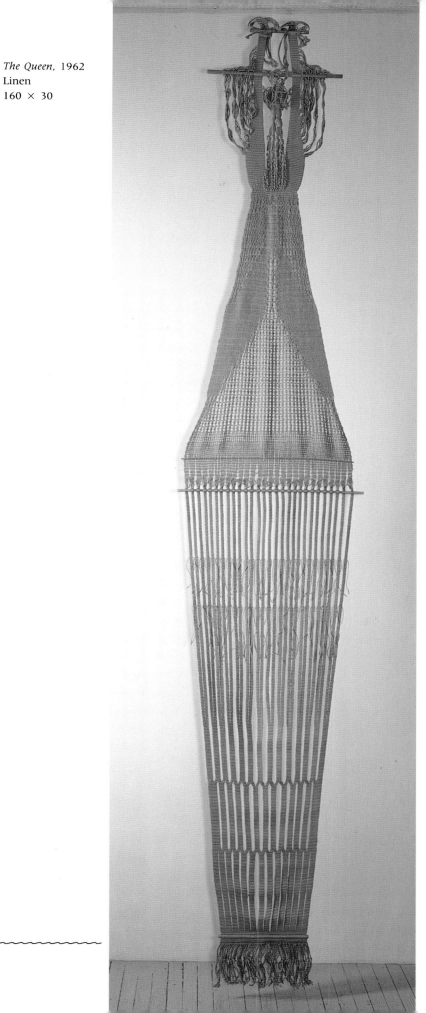

the Tao, a Path; the Way, the Absolute, the Law, Nature, Supreme Reason. Laotse says: "there is a thing which is all-containing, which was born before the existence of Heaven & Earth. How silent! How solitary! It stands alone & changes not. It revolves without danger to itself & is the mother of the universe. I do not know its name & so call it the Path.

The Path, 1962
Linen, 24k gold
$90\frac{1}{2} \times 24\frac{1}{2}$

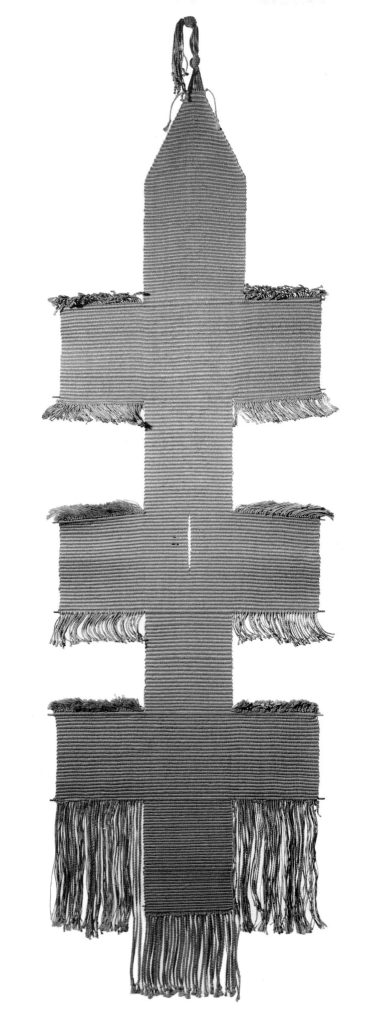

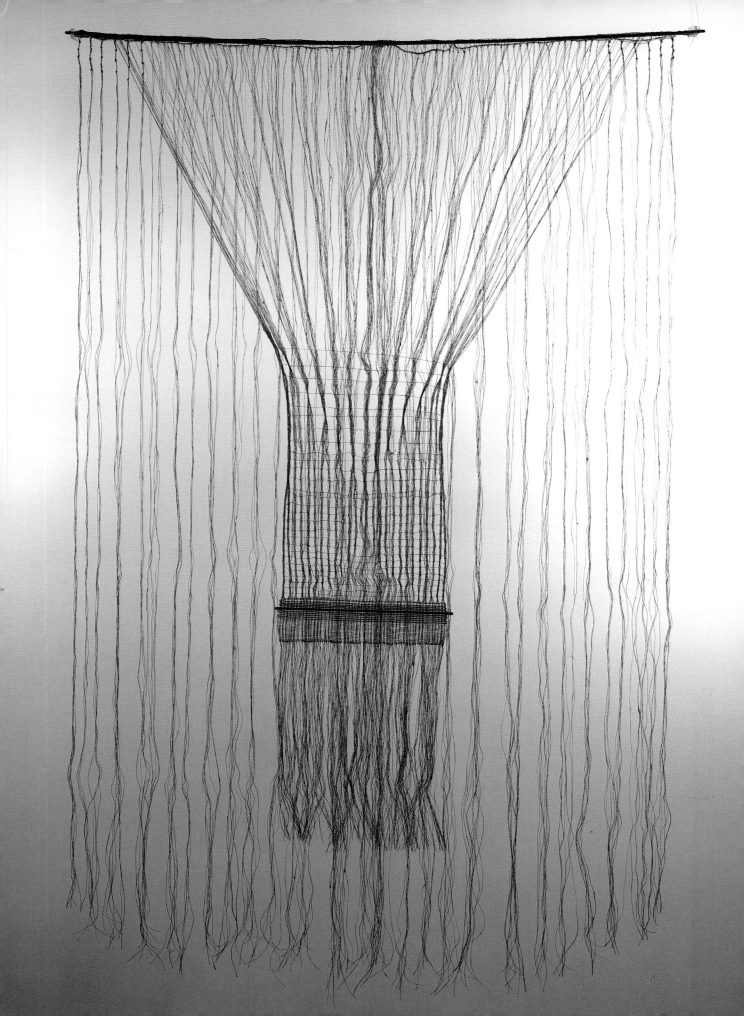

Lekythos, 1962
Linen
50 × 31 $\frac{3}{4}$ × 1 $\frac{3}{4}$

Mask, ca. 1967
Linen, pre-Columbian beads and shell, horsehair
19 × 6 $\frac{1}{2}$

Shield IV, 1966
Linen, pre-Columbian beads and shells
$13\frac{1}{2} \times 10\frac{1}{2}$

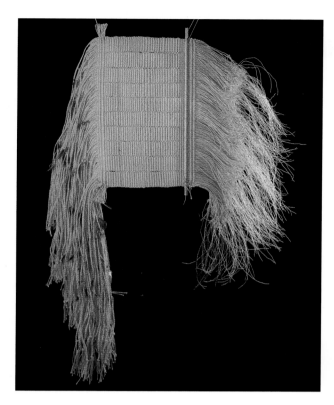

Shield, begun ca. 1967, completed 1985
Linen, silk, feathers
20 × 16

Shield, begun ca. 1967, completed 1989
Linen, feathers
$15\frac{1}{2} \times 6\frac{1}{2}$

Shield, begun ca. 1967, completed 1985
Linen, silk, feathers, whelk egg cases
$15\frac{1}{2} \times 14$

Tau, 1974
Linen
80 × 108

OPPOSITE:
Four Petaled Flower II, 1974
Linen
$87\frac{1}{2}$ × $84\frac{1}{2}$

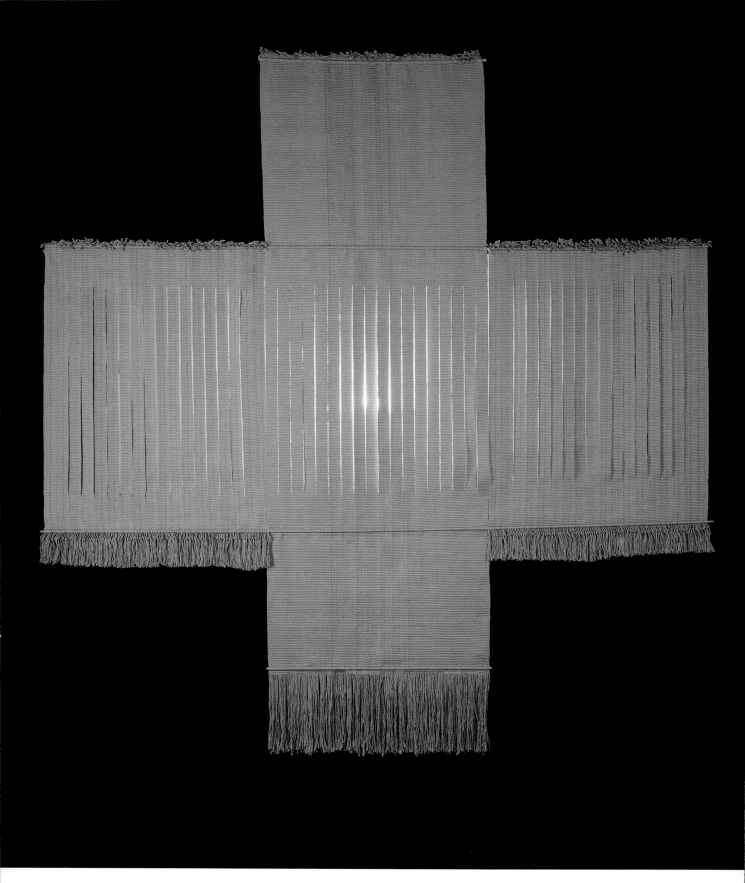

Dove, 1974
Linen
118 × 108

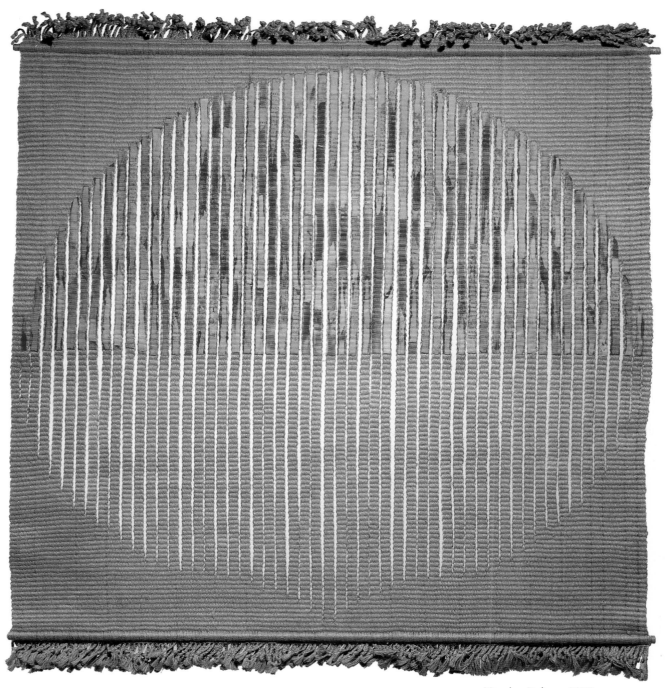

Morning Redness, 1974
Linen, manuscript paper, Liquitex
36 × 36

In Fields of Light, 1975
Linen
$108 \times 100\frac{1}{2}$

Red Sea, 1974
Linen
93 × 84

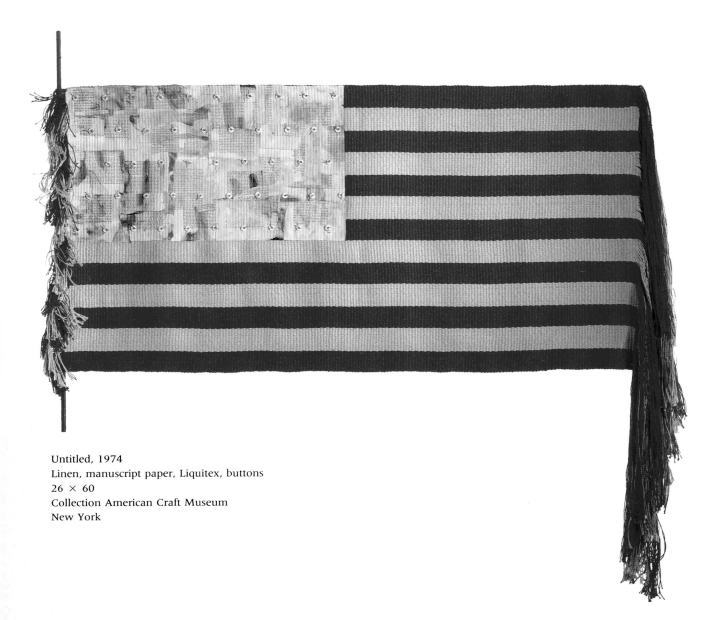

Untitled, 1974
Linen, manuscript paper, Liquitex, buttons
26 × 60
Collection American Craft Museum
New York

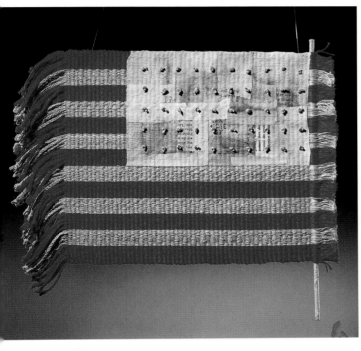

Untitled, 1974
Linen, manuscript paper, Liquitex
$14\frac{3}{4} \times 16\frac{1}{2}$

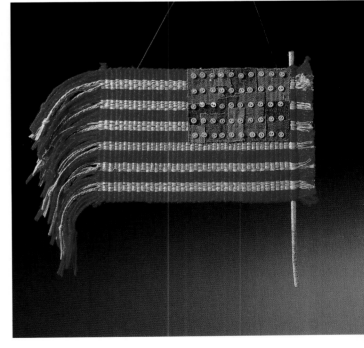

Untitled, 1974
Linen, denim, buttons
$7\frac{3}{4} \times 9\frac{3}{4}$

China – symbolic square of earth
+ its opposite
the perfect circle of the heavenly universe

The spherical or egg-shaped sky covered the earth, which was an egg-yolk lying in a liquid medium.

Or else the sky was a mobile canopy covering the earth in the shape of an inverted dish. The flat square surface of the dish lay directly below the peak of the canopy. Altars were therefore constructed in the image of this pyramidal universe + set within square buildings supporting a circular roof on four pillars.

Waters above the Firmament, 1976
Linen, manuscript paper, Liquitex
$156\frac{1}{2} \times 145\frac{1}{4}$
Collection The Art Institute of Chicago
Harriott A. Fox Endowment; Mrs. Siegfried G. Schmidt Endowment; H. L. and Mary T. Adams Endowment; restricted gift of the Textile Society of the Art Institute of Chicago; Laurance H. Armour, Jr. and Margot B. Armour Family Foundation; Mrs. William B. Swartchild, Jr.; Joan Rosenberg; Joseph Fell (1983.203). Photograph courtesy The Art Institute of Chicago.

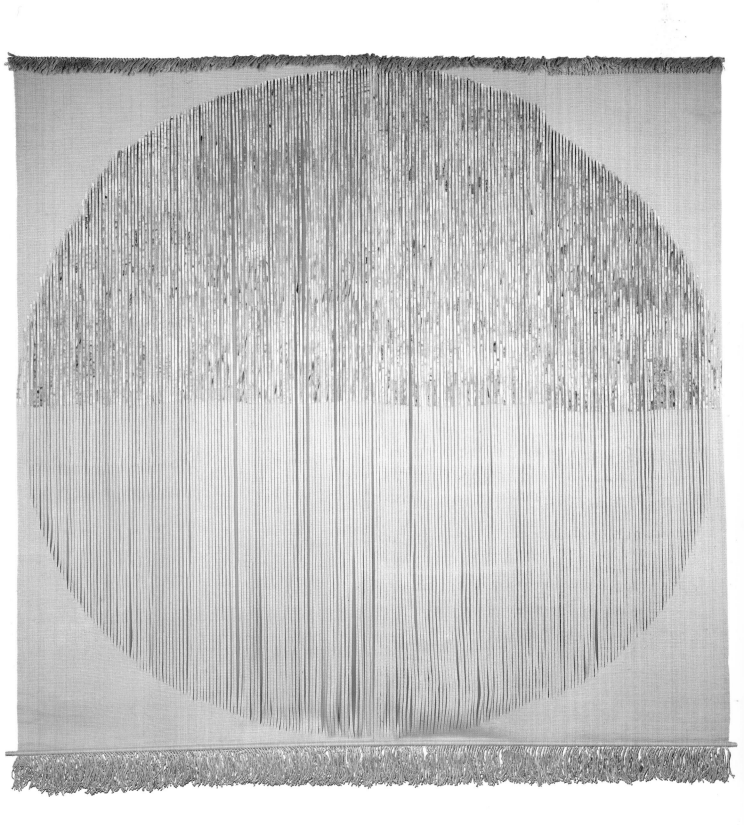

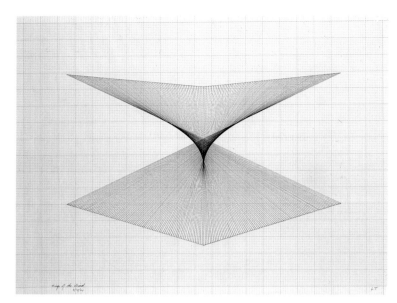

Wings of the Wind, 1964
India ink on graph paper
$17\frac{1}{2} \times 22\frac{1}{4}$

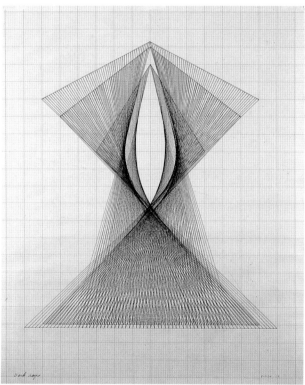

Dark Rays, 1964
India ink on graph paper
$22 \times 17\frac{1}{4}$

Region of Fire, 1964
India ink on graph paper
$23\frac{1}{4} \times 18\frac{1}{4}$

Union of Fire and Water, 1964
India ink on graph paper
23 × 18

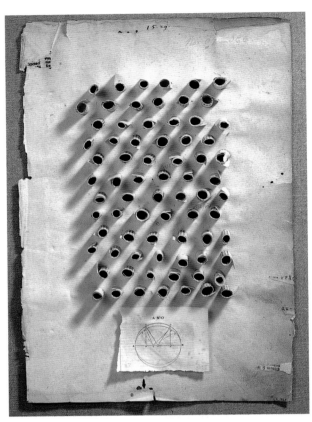

Ano, 1965
$16 \times 10\frac{3}{4} \times \frac{7}{8}$

Detail of *Ano,* 1965

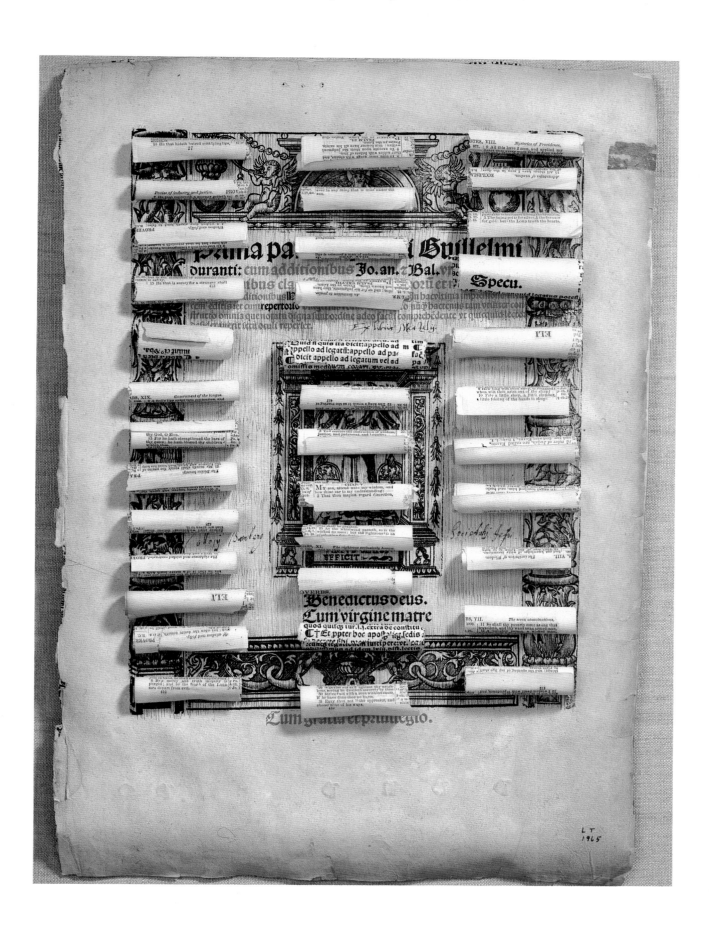

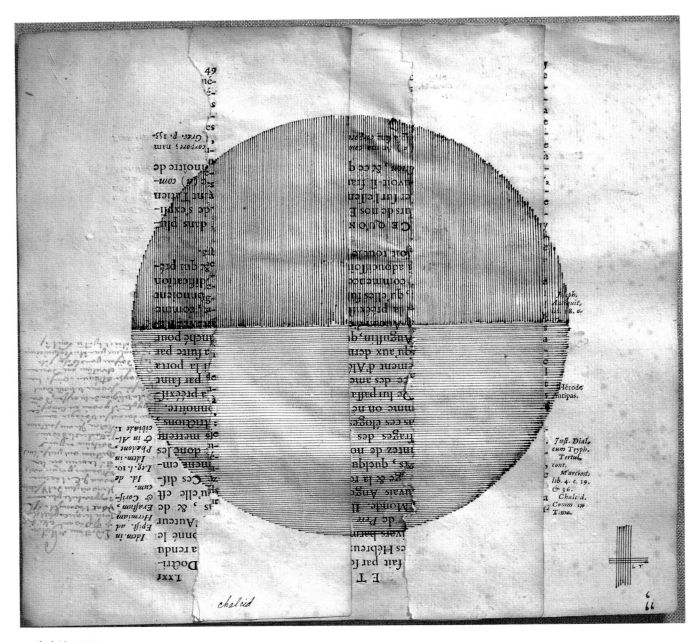

Chalcid, 1966

$9\frac{5}{8} \times 10\frac{1}{4}$

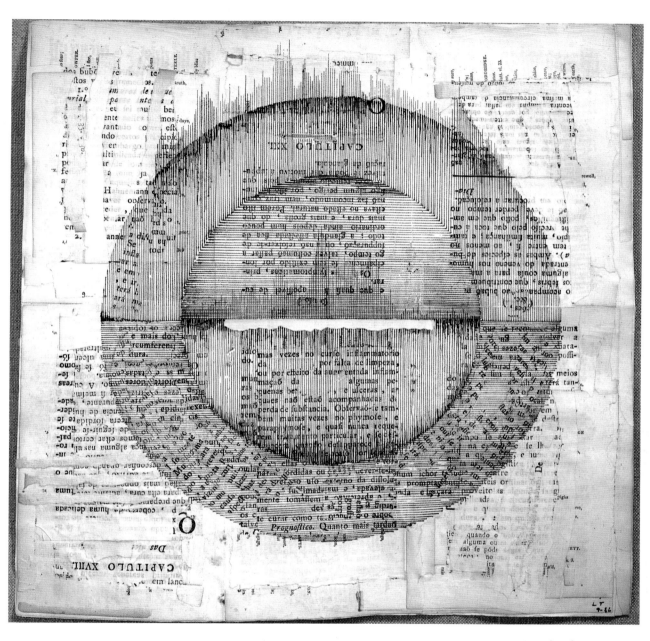

Round and Square, 1966
$10\frac{3}{4} \times 10\frac{3}{4}$

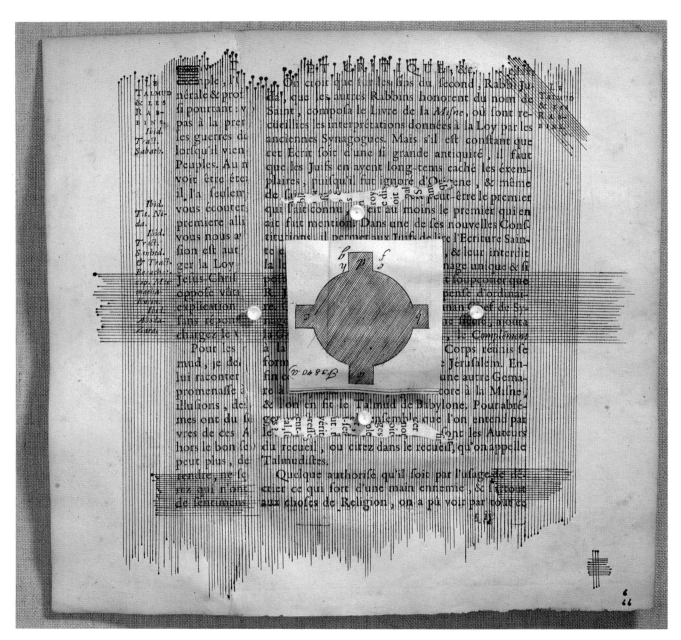

Discours Historiques, 1966
$9\frac{1}{2} \times 9\frac{3}{4} \times \frac{1}{8}$

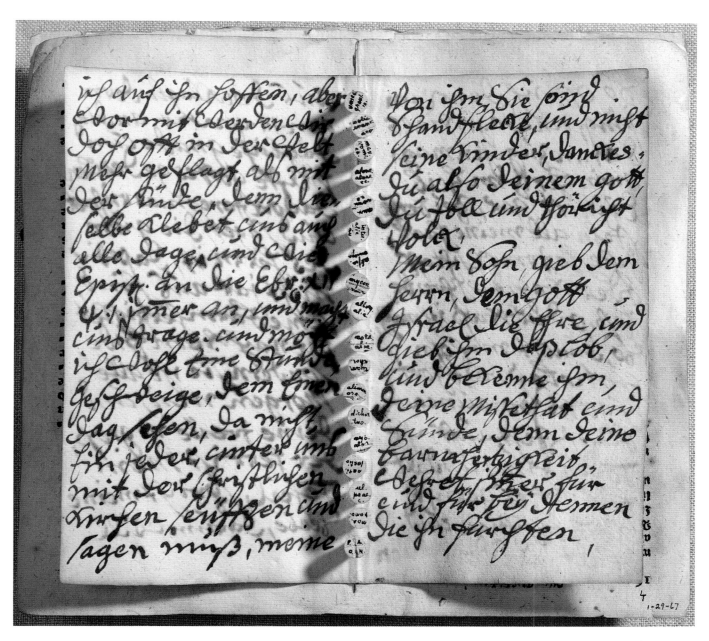

Epître, 1967
$7 \times 7 \frac{3}{4} \times 1\frac{1}{4}$

May 4. 1979

The more it changes, the more
it is the same, — French saying

The work changes in form &
even in content, but still
it is the same, Like the
ocean, the surface has waves &
storms over it, but the
depths remain always calm
dark, ~~mysterious~~, full of life
& mystery. We know not
what is in our depths.
So our life, transmuted into
our work.
"What artist would not wish to

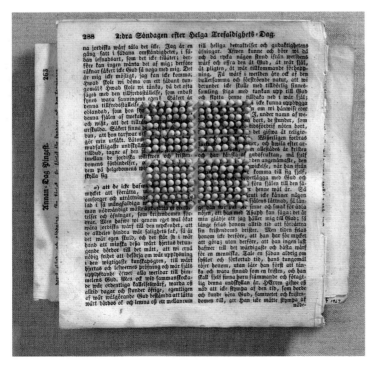

Deposits of Holy Cities, 1967
$10\frac{3}{4} \times 10\frac{3}{4} \times \frac{1}{4}$

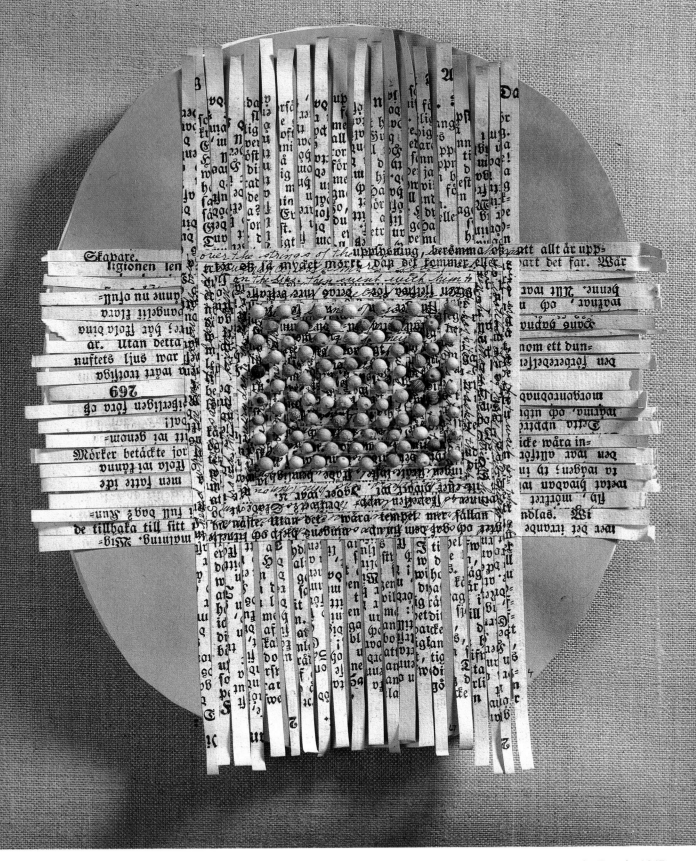

St. Francis, 1967
$8\frac{3}{4} \times 7\frac{1}{4} \times \frac{1}{4}$

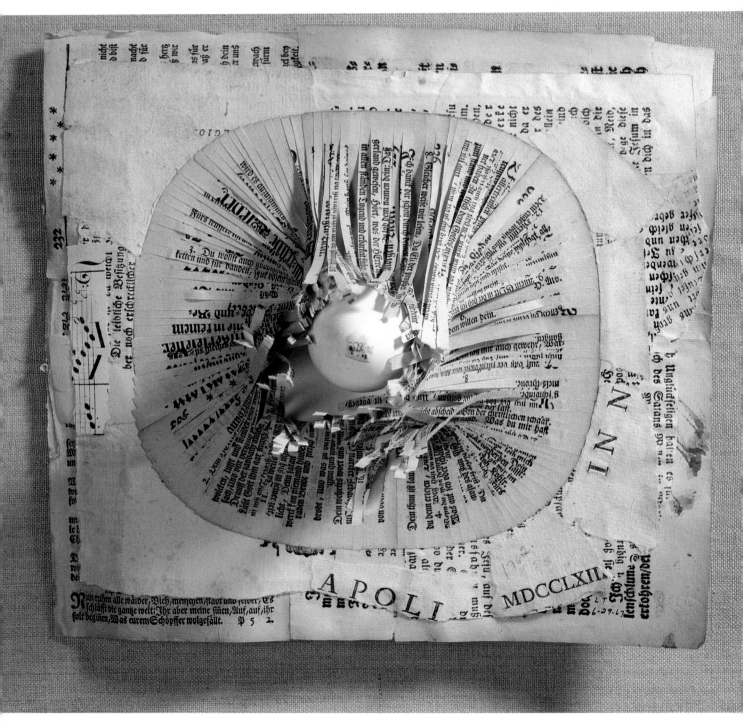

That Other Sea, 1967
$9 \times 8\frac{1}{4} \times 3\frac{1}{2}$

Distilla, 1967
$10\frac{1}{2} \times 8\frac{1}{4}$

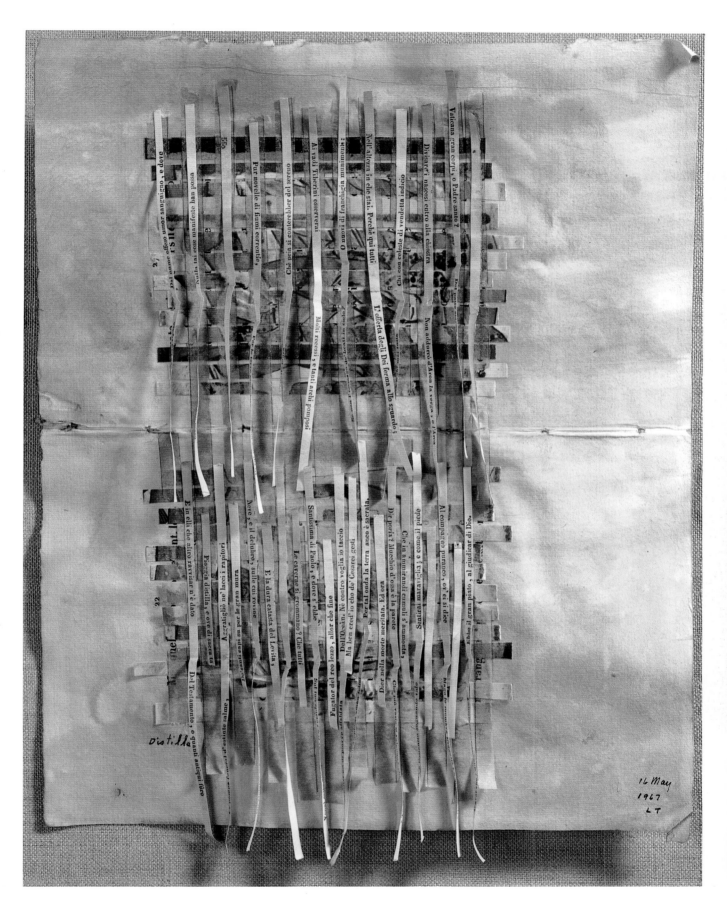

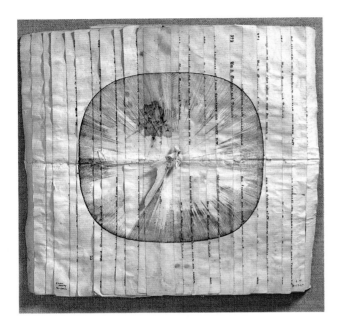

Green among the Bones, 1967
$9\frac{5}{8} \times 10\frac{5}{8} \times \frac{5}{8}$

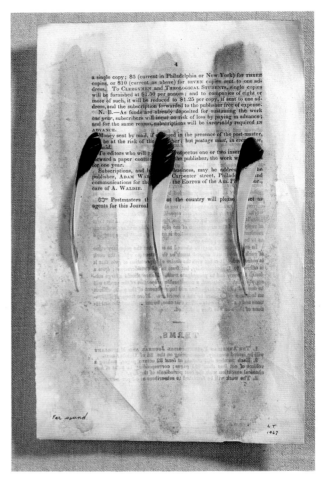

Far Sound, 1967
$9\frac{1}{4} \times 5\frac{3}{4} \times \frac{1}{4}$

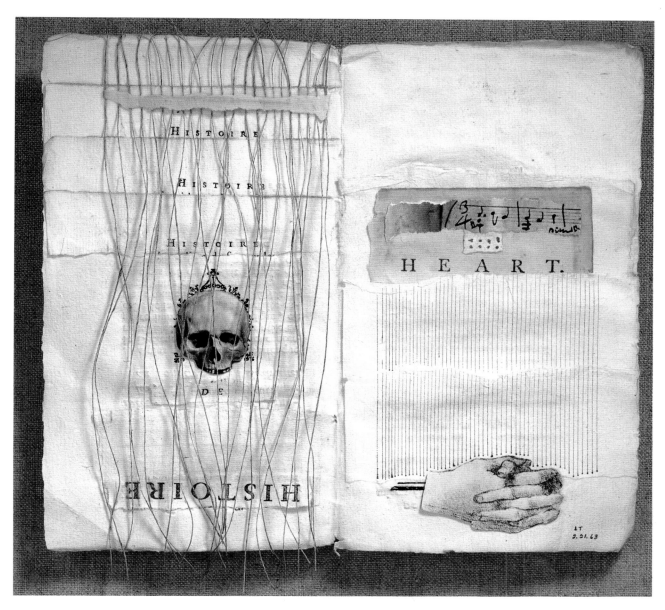

Heart, 1968
$8\frac{3}{8} \times 8\frac{1}{4}$

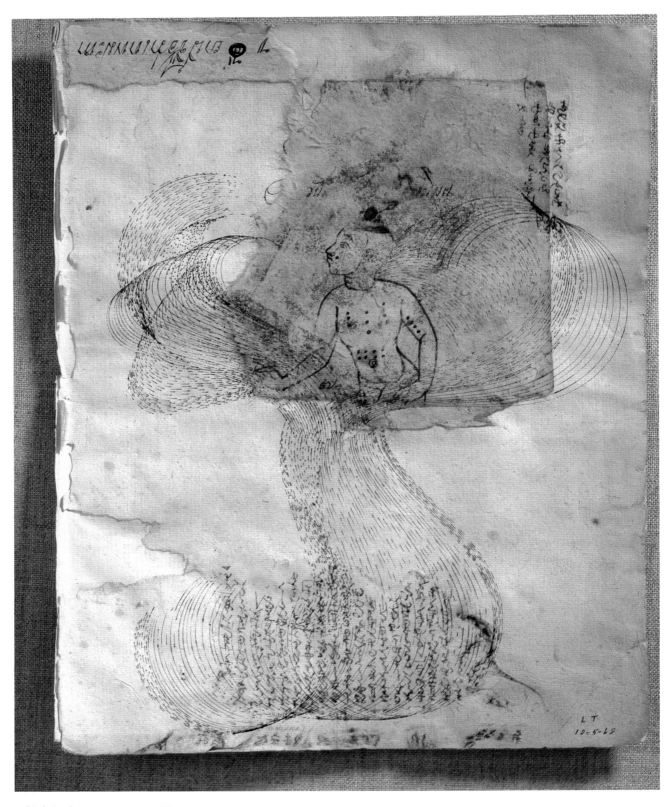

Rebirth in the Western Sea, 1968
$9\frac{3}{4} \times 7\frac{5}{8}$

Song on the Evening Hill, 1968
$11 \times 10\frac{5}{8} \times 2$

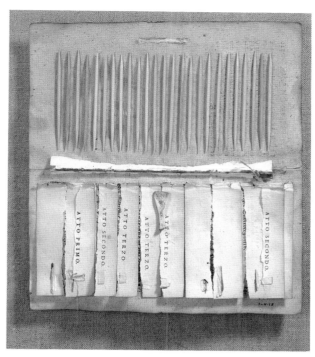

Rivers in the Sea, 1968
$10\frac{1}{2} \times 8\frac{1}{2}$

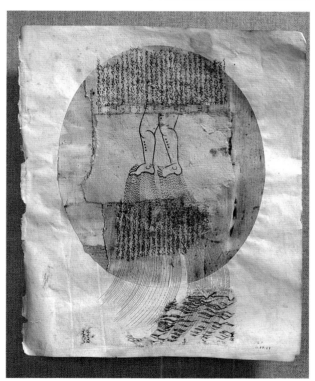

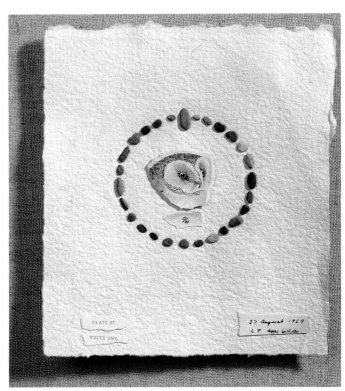

Plate 27, 1969
$5\frac{1}{2} \times 4\frac{3}{4} \times \frac{1}{8}$

Emblem of Infinity, 1969
$4 \times 5\frac{1}{2}$

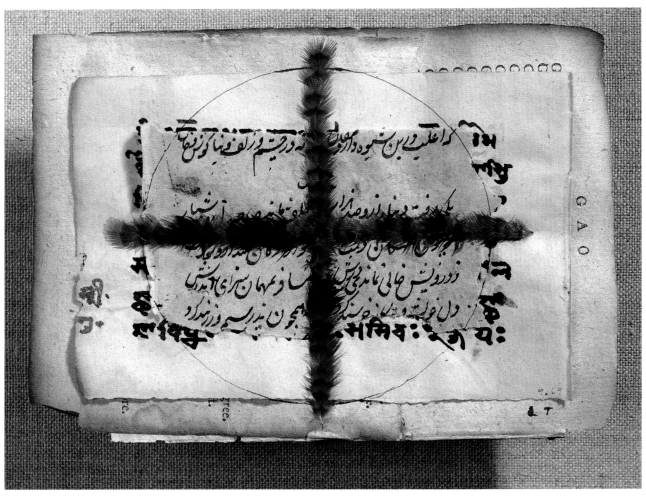

The Matrix, 1970
$6\frac{1}{2} \times 8 \times 1\frac{1}{2}$

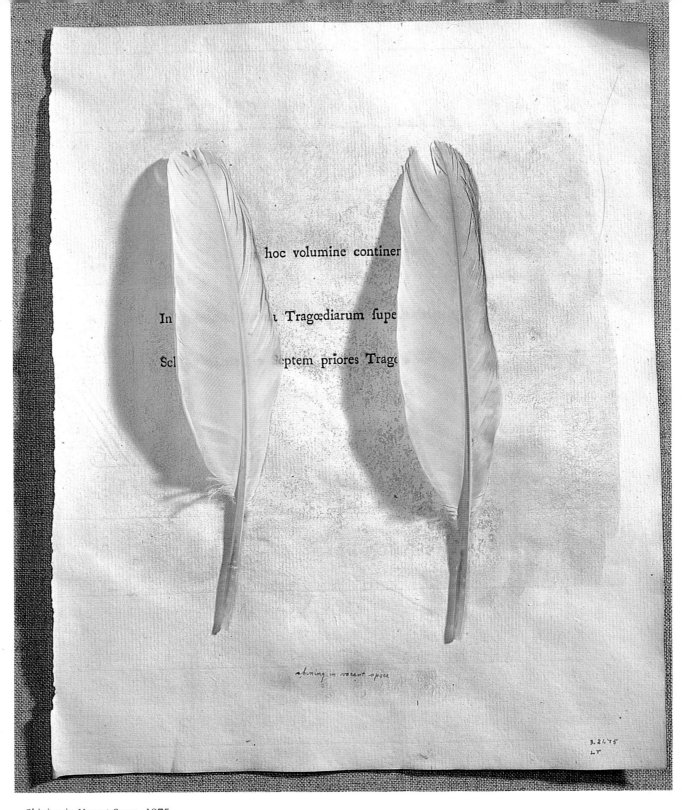

Shining in Vacant Space, 1975
$11\frac{1}{2} \times 9\frac{1}{8} \times 1$

Adulterated Flag, 1975
7 × 8¾

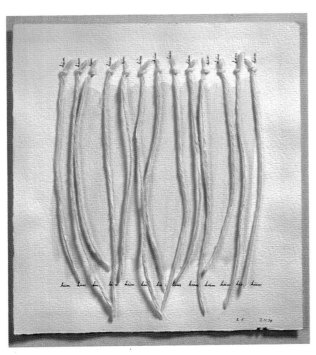

Peach Hum with Threads, 1979
$6\frac{1}{2} \times 7\frac{1}{2}$

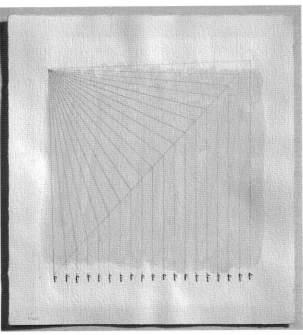

Peach Hum with Lines, 1980
$6\frac{1}{2} \times 7\frac{1}{2}$

the sacred seed-syllable
Hūm

Hūm is the infinite in the finite,
the eternal in the temporal, the
timeless in the moment, the
unconditioned in the conditioned,
the formless as basis for all form,
the transcendental in the
ephemeral; it is the Wisdom
of the Great Mirror, which
reflects the Void (*śūnyata*) as
much as the objects, & reveals
the 'emptiness' in the things
as much as the things in the
'emptiness'.

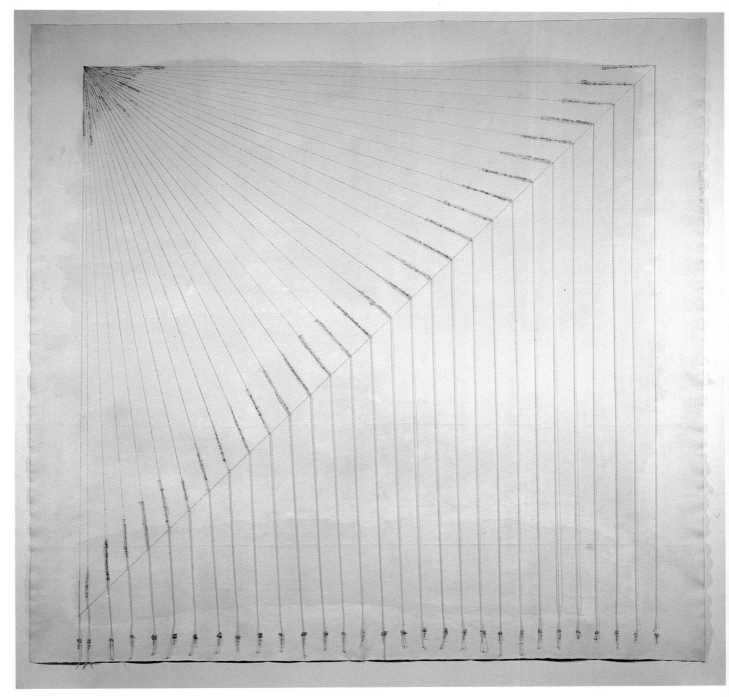

Hum, ca. 1986
$74\frac{3}{8} \times 75\frac{3}{8}$

Manuscript Writing, 1980

$7 \times 8\frac{3}{8}$

words & letters can be compacted
to a dense knot or drawn out
to great length; can be angular
or curving; can be small or large

major artistic vehicle of
a great civilization

hand-writing: brocade woven
by the calamus with the thread
of discernment - *Ars Islamica*

O Crystalline Fount (Eyes Series II), 1982
$6\frac{3}{8} \times 6\frac{1}{4}$

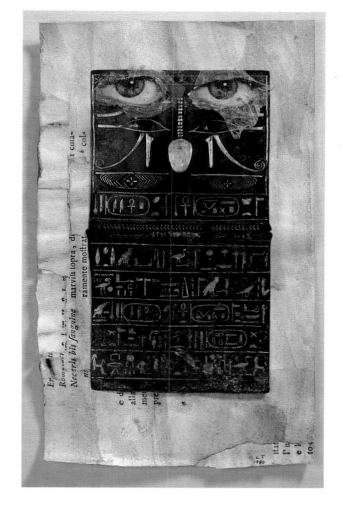

Untitled *(Eyes Series I)*, 1980
$9\frac{1}{2} \times 5\frac{3}{4}$

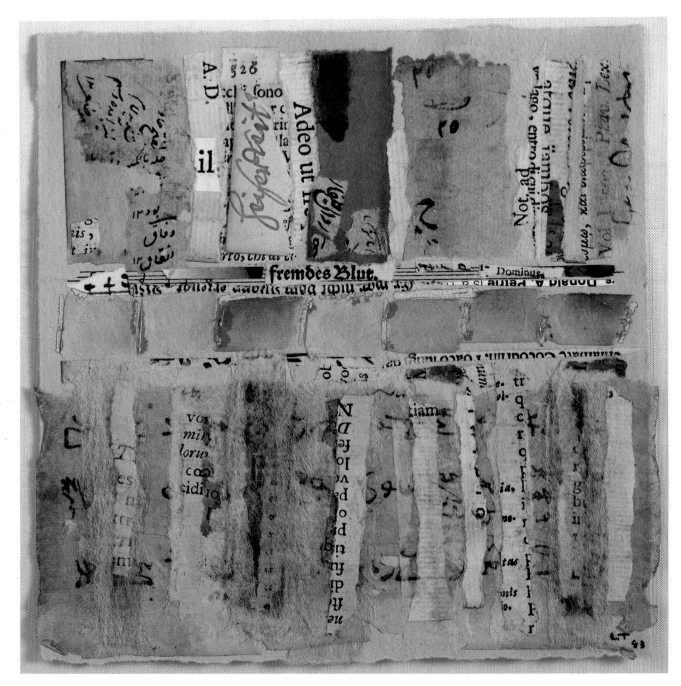

Untitled, 1983
$5\frac{1}{2} \times 5\frac{3}{8}$

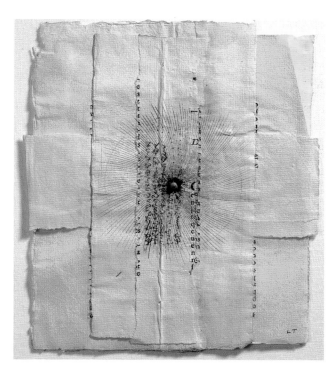

The First Dust of Spring, ca. 1984
$7\frac{1}{4} \times 6\frac{1}{8}$

Your Glance Scatters Leaves, ca. 1984
$4 \times 5\frac{3}{4}$

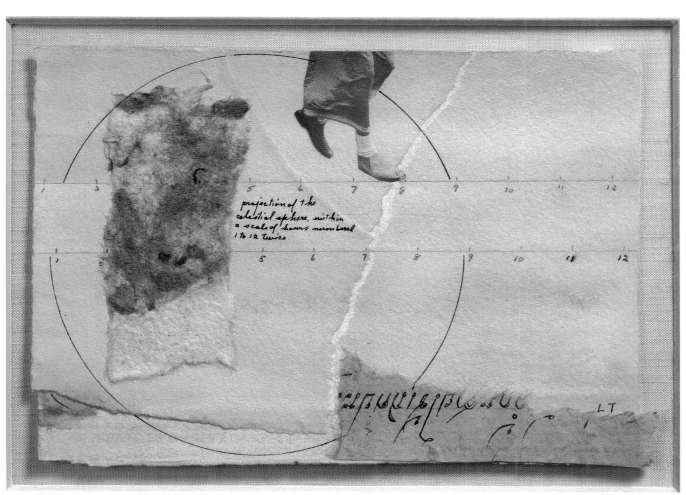

Untitled, 1985
$6\frac{5}{8} \times 7\frac{1}{2}$

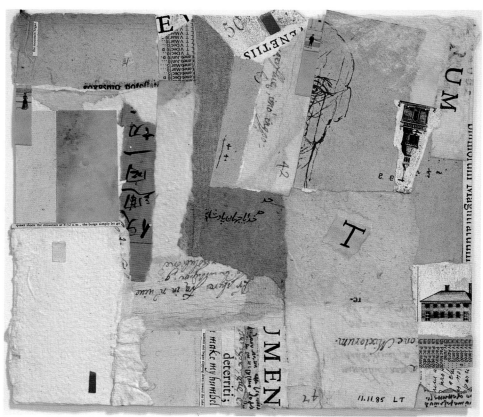

Schwitters' Smile, 1985
7 × 9

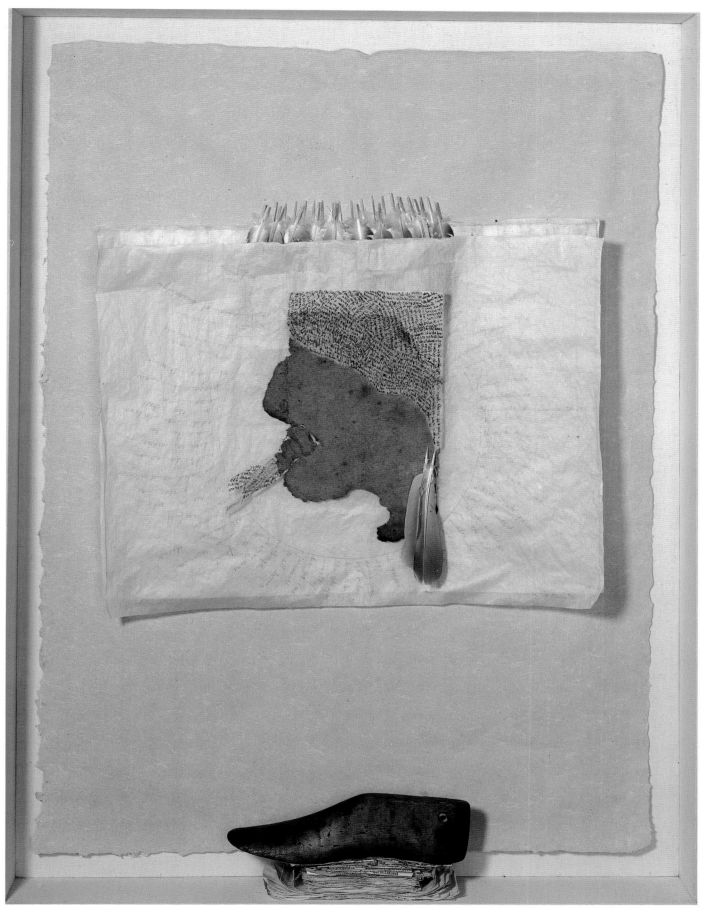

The Via Sancta, 1985
35 × 26½ × 4⅛

Detail of *Upon a Grey Shore*, 1986

Upon a Grey Shore, 1986
$41 \times 30\frac{1}{2} \times 6\frac{1}{4}$

To Goethe color was the voice of God
                              speaking thru Nature
Blackness was not merely an absence of light,
it was the background of the cosmos, a
field of intense activity for Beings of a
vastly higher order than humanity

Collection of postcard collages, 1966–86
Approximately 4 × 6 each
Collection Diana Epstein and Millicent Safro

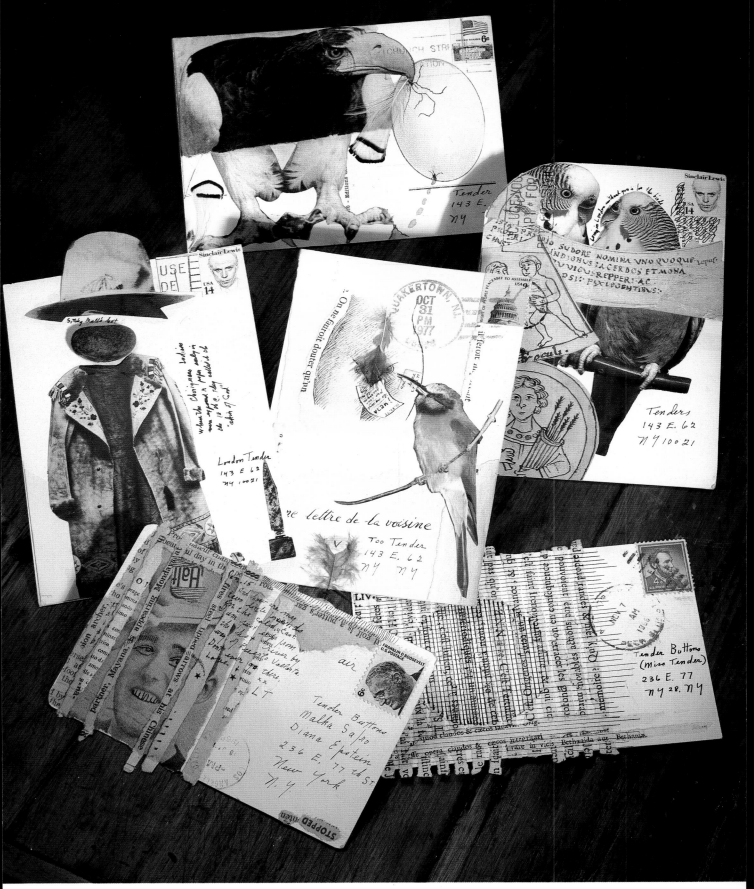

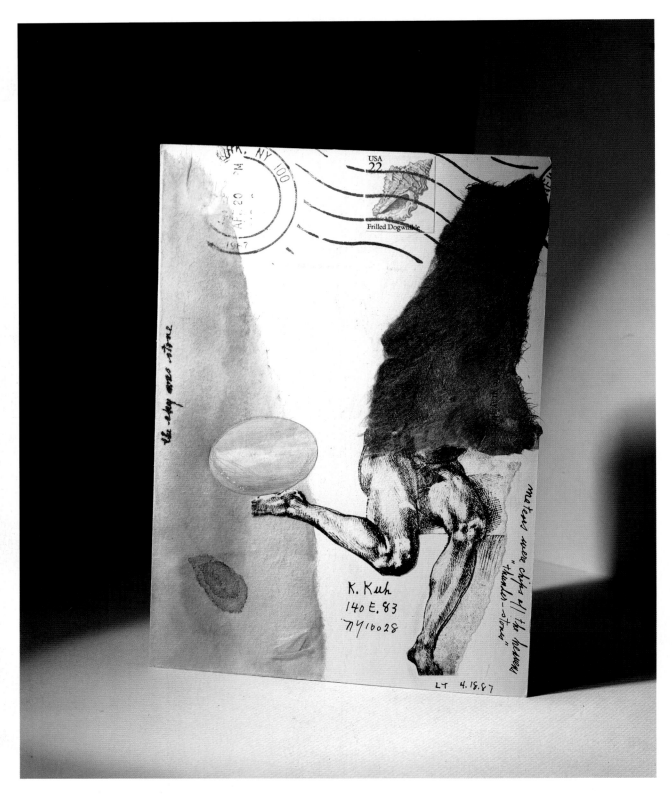

Postcard collage, 1987
4 × 6
Collection Katharine Kuh

Postcard collage, 1971
4 × 6
Collection Diana Epstein and Millicent Safro

Creatures, 1985
$4\frac{1}{4} \times 5\frac{5}{8} \times 1\frac{5}{8}$ (closed)

Windows, 1985
$5\frac{1}{4} \times 3\frac{3}{4} \times 2\frac{3}{4}$ (closed)

Supreme, begun ca. 1974, completed 1984
46×15
Collection Edna S. Beron

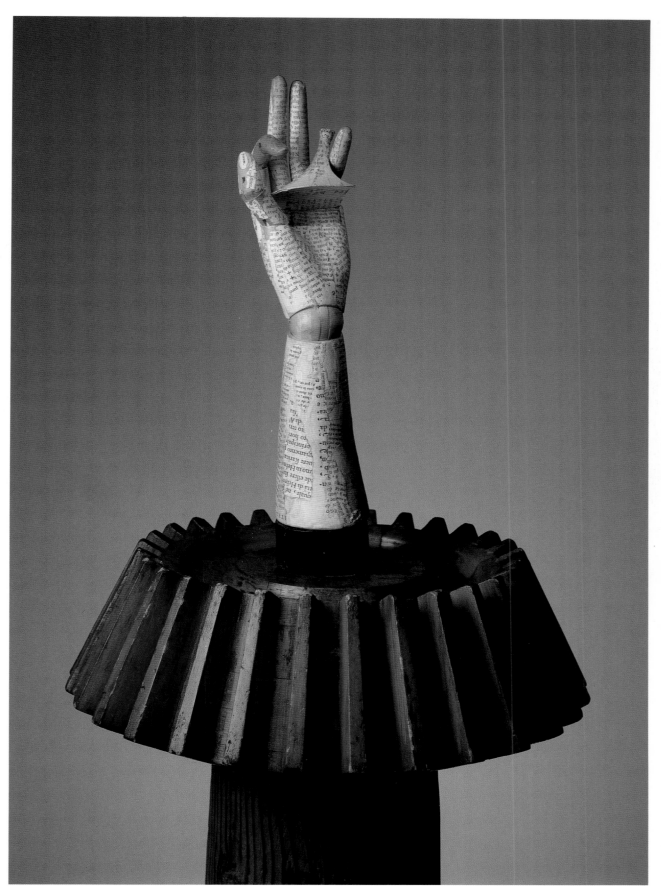

Médecins Anciens, 1966
$2\frac{1}{2} \times 8\frac{1}{2} \times 5\frac{1}{4}$

Materia Medica, 1967
$2\frac{1}{4} \times 9\frac{1}{4} \times 5\frac{3}{4}$

Detail of *Médecins Anciens*, 1966

Even Thread Had a Speech, 1966
$5 \times 5\frac{1}{4} \times 2\frac{1}{4}$

Seed Puzzle on Three Levels, 1966
$7\frac{7}{8} \times 5\frac{7}{8} \times 3\frac{1}{2}$

Pia Avis, 1969
$6\frac{1}{4} \times 6\frac{3}{8} \times 4\frac{3}{4}$

Sept. 22, 1968 - first day of Autumn
(the seasons come
with their gifts)

"To have original, extraordinary, & perhaps even immortal ideas, one has but to isolate oneself from the world for a few moments so completely that the most commonplace happenings appear to be new & unfamiliar, & in this way reveal their true essence."

Schopenhauer

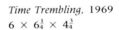

Time Trembling, 1969
$6 \times 6\frac{1}{4} \times 4\frac{3}{4}$

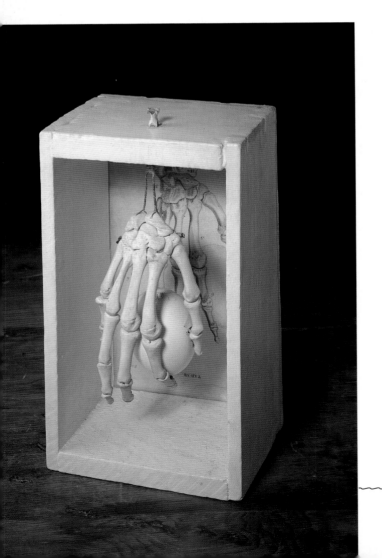

A Dry Cry from the Desert, 1970
$9\frac{1}{2} \times 5\frac{1}{2} \times 4\frac{3}{4}$

The struggle to express an inner
vision of a reality greater than
the individual self, a reality
that transcends the mundane, is
what lies at the root of a genuine
artistic impulse.

C. G. Jung

Detail of *Udjat,* 1968

Udjat, 1968
$2 \times 7\frac{1}{4} \times 5\frac{1}{2}$

And the Sound Is the Sound of the Sea, 1964
$1\frac{3}{8} \times 8\frac{1}{2} \times 5\frac{1}{8}$

These Words in Sand, 1968
$2\frac{3}{4} \times 8\frac{1}{2} \times 5\frac{1}{8}$

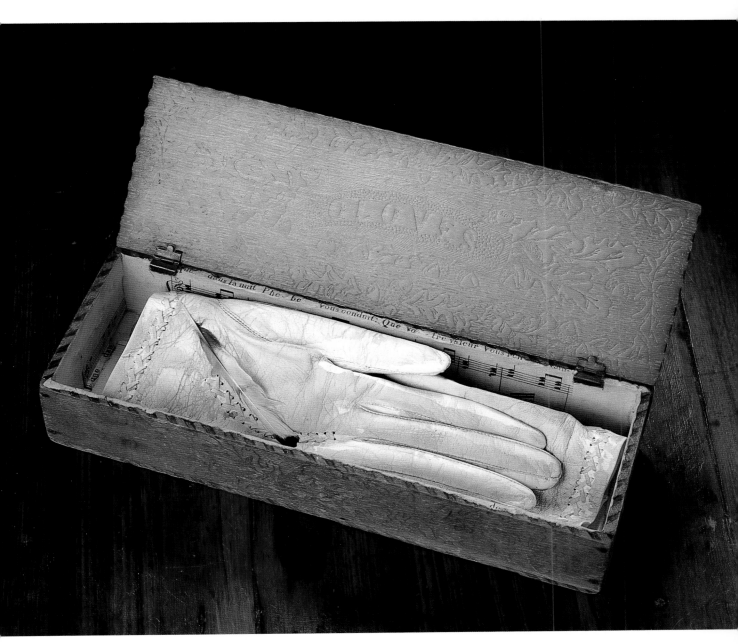

Birth, 1970
$2 \times 10\frac{1}{8} \times 3\frac{1}{2}$

The Fairest of Plants, 1969
$7 \times 7\frac{1}{4} \times 5\frac{1}{4}$

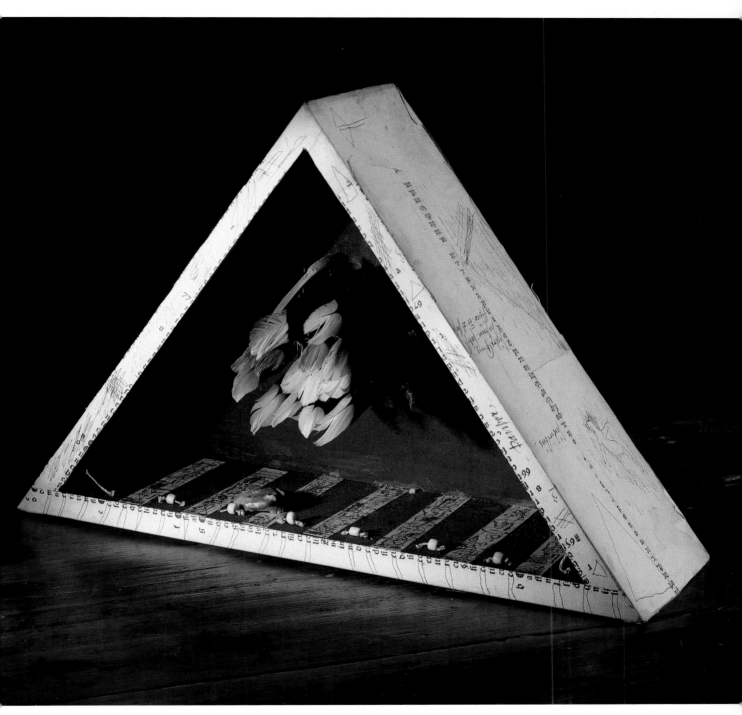

Ode to a Sparrow, 1987
$8 \times 11\frac{7}{8} \times 3\frac{1}{4}$

Feather Music, 1987
$3\frac{3}{8} \times 2 \times 4$

Feather Music, 1987
$5\frac{3}{4} \times 2\frac{1}{2} \times 4$

Feather Music, ca. 1967
$5\frac{1}{2} \times 2 \times 4$

Or to an Illegible Stone, 1989
$3 \times 8\frac{3}{8} \times 7\frac{1}{4}$

Dark Music, 1972–74
$9\frac{3}{4} \times 3\frac{3}{8} \times 6$

Easter Breakfast, 1982
$3\frac{1}{4} \times 7\frac{3}{4}$ diam.

Half Heard, in the Stillness, 1989
$4\frac{3}{4} \times 11\frac{1}{2} \times 5\frac{1}{8}$

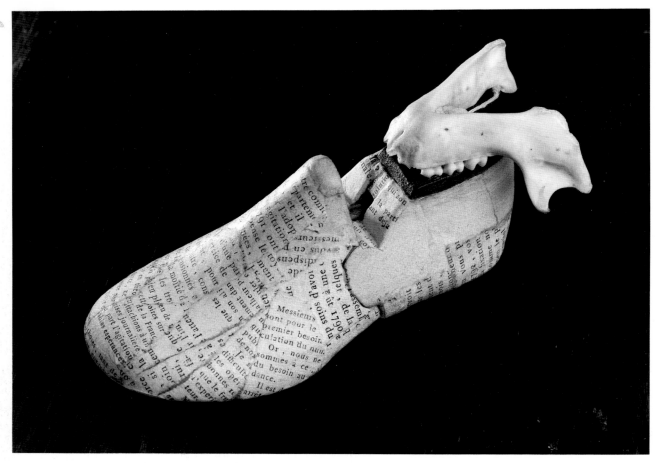

Celestial Messenger, 1978
$2\frac{1}{4} \times 5\frac{1}{4} \times 2\frac{1}{4}$

What artist would not wish to dwell there — in the bosom of nature, in the primordial source of creation, where the secret key of everything is kept? But not all are meant to reach it. Our instinct drives us downward, deep down to the primal source, ... then we have visionary experiences made visible.

K lee

Foot Forms, 1984–86
$2\frac{1}{4} \times 5\frac{1}{2} \times 2\frac{1}{4}$ each

Detail of *Collage Chest*, begun 1974

Collage Chest, work in progress, begun 1974
$37\frac{1}{4} \times 21\frac{1}{4} \times 22$
Courtesy Helen Drutt Gallery
New York and Philadelphia

Collage Chest II, work in progress, begun 1974
$13\frac{1}{8} \times 5\frac{3}{8} \times 11\frac{1}{4}$

Wounded Duck, 1984
$5\frac{3}{4} \times 14\frac{1}{8} \times 4$

I am seeking for the bridge which leads from the visible to the invisible, like the famous cabalist who once said "If you wish to get hold of the invisible you must penetrate as deeply as possible into the visible."

Max Beckmann

... the inner recesses of the heart; that corner which is the most profound & the most mysterious, & finally the truest, to look only into this corner & to see only through this corner

G. de Chirico

In Utero, 1985
48 × 48 × 48
Photograph by John Bigelow Taylor

Catalogue of the Exhibition

All dimensions are given in inches, and are listed in order of height, width, and depth. Unless otherwise noted, all loans are courtesy of the artist.

SCULPTURE

Representative of Tawney's early work in clay, these sculptures were created while she was a student of Alexander Archipenko.

**1. Untitled, ca. 1947–48
Fired clay
$9\frac{3}{4} \times 8\frac{1}{2} \times 4\frac{1}{2}$
Collection Mrs. Jack Weinberg

**2. Untitled, ca. 1947–48
Fired clay
$13 \times 7 \times 3\frac{1}{2}$
Collection Mrs. Jack Weinberg

**3. Untitled, ca. 1947–48
Fired clay
$13\frac{3}{4} \times 4 \times 2$
Collection Mrs. Jack Weinberg

Lenore Tawney working on *Waters above the Firmament*, Wooster Street studio, 1976.

FIBER

Tawney's early works in fiber, catalogue numbers 4 through 13, illustrate her exploration of plain and tapestry weaves and her open-warp weaving. Numbers 14 through 16 represent her work in gauze weave. The woven forms, numbers 17–21, 26–28, and 36–37, demonstrate Tawney's invention and her original combination of several techniques. Still based upon gauze weave, these works were woven using Tawney's open reed. Here, she combined areas of warp-faced plain weave with double wefts with slit tapestry, braiding, and knotting. The shields, squares, and masks, numbers 22–25 and 29–35, are woven in warp-faced plain weave with double wefts. They are characterized by extensive braiding, wrapping, and knotting. The monumental squares and crosses and the flags, numbers 38 through 48, are also woven in warp-faced plain weave with double wefts. Many of these works

*New York only
**New York and Chicago only
***Chicago only

incorporate slit tapestry, collage elements, braiding, and knotting. In the clouds, numbers 49 and 50, linen threads are suspended from canvas supports in a grid pattern.

4. *St. Francis and the Birds,* 1954
   Wool
   $32\frac{1}{2} \times 17\frac{1}{2}$

5. *Bound Man,* 1957
   Wool, silk, linen, goathair
   84×36
   Collection American Craft Museum
   New York

6. *Lost and Proud,* 1957
   Linen, wool, silk
   $43 \times 51\frac{1}{2}$

7. *Yellows,* 1958
   Wool, linen
   $84 \times 50\frac{1}{2}$

***8. *Landscape,* 1958
   Silk, cotton, linen, synthetic fibers
   $56\frac{1}{8} \times 26\frac{1}{4}$
   Collection The Art Institute of Chicago
   Alexander Demond Endowment (1981.37)

9. *Jupiter,* 1959
   Wool, silk
   53×41
   Collection American Craft Museum
   New York
   Gift of the Johnson Wax Company,
   from Objects: USA

**10. *Two Forces Meeting and Opposing,* 1959
   Linen, wool, silk, rayon, nylon, acetate
   $75\frac{1}{8} \times 31\frac{3}{8}$
   Collection The Art Institute of Chicago
   Restricted gift of Mrs. Tiffany Blake and
   Textile Study Room Fund (1969.97)

11. *Triune,* 1961
   Linen, wool, silk
   $109\frac{1}{2} \times 104$
   Collection The Metropolitan Museum of Art
   New York
   Purchase, the Louis Comfort Tiffany
   Foundation Gift, 1983 (1983.22)

12. *Owls,* ca. 1961
   Linen, wool, graphite
   $41 \times 10\frac{1}{2}$

13. *Owl,* ca. 1961
   Linen, wool
   $44 \times 17\frac{1}{2}$
   Collection Mrs. Jack Weinberg

14. *Seed,* 1961
   Linen, cotton, wool
   88×19
   Collection Cooper-Hewitt
   National Museum of Design,
   Smithsonian Institution
   New York

15. *The Judge,* 1961
   Linen
   124×14

16. *Vespers,* 1961
   Linen
   82×21

17. *The King I,* 1962
   Linen
   148×31

18. *The Queen,* 1962
   Linen
   160×30

19. *Dark River,* 1962
   Linen, wood
   $163 \times 22\frac{1}{2}$
   Collection The Museum of Modern Art
   New York
   Greta Daniel Design Fund

20. *The Path,* 1962
   Linen, 24k gold
   $90\frac{1}{2} \times 24\frac{1}{2}$

21. *Lekythos,* 1962
   Linen
   $50 \times 31\frac{3}{4} \times 1\frac{1}{4}$

22. *Shield II,* 1963
Linen, feathers, porcupine quills
24 × 16
Collection American Craft Museum
New York
Gift of the Dreyfus Corporation

23. *Bird Square II,* 1963
Linen, feathers
$7\frac{1}{2}$ × $5\frac{1}{4}$
Collection Cooper-Hewitt National Museum
of Design,
Smithsonian Institution
New York

24. *Cross,* 1964
Linen
20 × 15
Collection Cooper-Hewitt National Museum
of Design,
Smithsonian Institution
New York

25. *Bird,* ca. 1965
Linen, feathers
32 × 18
Collection Ted Hallman

***26. *Underwater Wind,* 1965
Linen, silk, wood, feathers
48 × 16
Collection The Art Institute of Chicago
Gift of Katharine Kuh (1988.517)

27. *Inside the Earth, a Mountain,* ca. 1965
Linen
103 × $16\frac{1}{2}$ × $2\frac{3}{4}$

28. *Black Woven Form (Fountain),* 1966
Linen
103 × $15\frac{1}{4}$
Collection American Craft Museum
New York

29. *Shield IV,* 1966
Linen, pre-Columbian beads and shells
$13\frac{1}{2}$ × $10\frac{1}{2}$

30. *A Faint Aroma of Snow,* 1967
Linen, gold leaf
11 × 6
Collection Alex and Camille Cook

31. *Mask,* ca. 1967
Linen, pre-Columbian beads and shell, horsehair
19 × $6\frac{1}{2}$

**32. *Mask with Horsehair,* ca. 1967
Linen, horsehair, gold, pre-Columbian beads
24 × 8
Collection The Art Institute of Chicago
Restricted gift of Mrs. Tiffany Blake in honor of
Mrs. John V. Farwell III (1969.108)

33. *Shield,* begun ca. 1967, completed 1985
Linen, silk, feathers
20 × 16

34. *Shield,* begun ca. 1967, completed 1985
Linen, silk, feathers, whelk egg cases
$15\frac{1}{2}$ × 14

35. *Shield,* begun ca. 1967, completed 1989
Linen, feathers
$15\frac{1}{2}$ × $6\frac{1}{2}$

36. *Orinoco,* 1967
Linen
129 × $22\frac{1}{2}$ × 4

37. *Little River II,* ca. 1969
Linen
$92\frac{1}{2}$ × $27\frac{1}{4}$
Collection American Craft Museum
New York
Gift of the Dreyfus Corporation

38. *Waters above the Firmament,* 1974
Linen, manuscript paper, Liquitex
36 × 36
Collection The First National Bank of Chicago

39. *Morning Redness,* 1974
Linen, manuscript paper, Liquitex
36 × 36

~~~~~~~~~~~~~~~

*New York only
**New York and Chicago only
***Chicago only

40. *Tau*, 1974
Linen
80 × 108

41. *Four Petaled Flower II*, 1974
Linen
$87\frac{1}{2} \times 84\frac{1}{2}$

42. *Dove*, 1974
Linen
118 × 108

43. *Red Sea*, 1974
Linen
93 × 84

44. Untitled, 1974
Linen, manuscript paper, Liquitex, buttons
26 × 60
Collection American Craft Museum
New York

45. Untitled, 1974
Linen, denim, buttons
$7\frac{3}{4} \times 9\frac{3}{4}$

46. Untitled, 1974
Linen, manuscript paper, Liquitex
$14\frac{3}{4} \times 16\frac{1}{2}$

47. *In Fields of Light*, 1975
Linen
$108 \times 100\frac{1}{2}$

***48. *Waters above the Firmament*, 1976
Linen, manuscript paper, Liquitex
$156\frac{1}{2} \times 145\frac{1}{4}$
Collection The Art Institute of Chicago
Harriott A. Fox Endowment; Mrs. Siegfried G.
Schmidt Endowment; H. L. and Mary T. Adams
Endowment; restricted gift of the Textile Society of
The Art Institute of Chicago; Laurance H. Armour,
Jr. and Margot B. Armour Family Foundation;
Mrs. William B. Swartchild, Jr.; Joan Rosenberg;
Joseph Fell (1983.203)

49. *Cloud Sculpture*, 1981
Canvas, linen
144 × 84 × 84
Collection American Craft Museum
New York
Gift of Richard Gonzales, in memory
of Lorraine Gonzales

*50. *Cloud Sculpture*, 1983
Canvas, linen
192 × 240 × 216

DRAWINGS

From a series of drawings done in 1964, these pieces were
inspired by Tawney's study of the Jacquard loom.

51. *Wings of the Wind*, 1964
India ink on graph paper
$17\frac{1}{2} \times 22\frac{1}{4}$

52. *Union of Fire and Water*, 1964
India ink on graph paper
23 × 18

53. *Dark Rays*, 1964
India ink on graph paper
$22 \times 17\frac{1}{4}$

54. *Region of Fire*, 1964
India ink on graph paper
$23\frac{1}{4} \times 18\frac{1}{4}$

COLLAGES

Tawney's collages incorporate such elements as the pages
of rare manuscripts in many languages, bones, feathers,
blown eggshells, and stones, and they are often enriched
by her own fine handwriting. Although these works are
generally intimate in scale, the collage paintings of the
1980s, numbers 78 and 93, are monumental. Numbers 94
through 96 represent the highly personal postcard collages
sent to friends, and 87 and 88 are books—with each page
an individual collage conceived as part of the whole.

55. *Ano*, 1965
$16 \times 10\frac{3}{4} \times \frac{7}{8}$

56. *Scrolls of the Law*, 1965
$16\frac{1}{4} \times 11\frac{1}{4} \times \frac{7}{8}$

57. *Chalcid*, 1966
$9\frac{5}{8} \times 10\frac{1}{4}$

58. *Round and Square*, 1966
$10\frac{3}{4} \times 10\frac{3}{4}$

59. *Discours Historiques*, 1966
$9\frac{1}{2} \times 9\frac{3}{4} \times \frac{1}{8}$

60. *Epître*, 1967
$7 \times 7\frac{3}{4} \times 1\frac{1}{4}$

61. *St. Francis*, 1967
$8\frac{3}{4} \times 7\frac{1}{4} \times \frac{1}{4}$

62. *Deposits of Holy Cities*, 1967
$10\frac{3}{4} \times 10\frac{3}{4} \times \frac{1}{4}$

*63. *That Other Sea*, 1967
$9 \times 8\frac{1}{4} \times 3\frac{1}{2}$

64. *Distilla*, 1967
$10\frac{1}{2} \times 8\frac{1}{4}$

65. *Green among the Bones*, 1967
$9\frac{5}{8} \times 10\frac{5}{8} \times \frac{5}{8}$

66. *Far Sound*, 1967
$9\frac{1}{4} \times 5\frac{3}{4} \times \frac{1}{4}$

67. *Heart*, 1968
$8\frac{3}{8} \times 8\frac{1}{4}$

68. *Song on the Evening Hill*, 1968
$11 \times 10\frac{5}{8} \times 2$

69. *Rivers in the Sea*, 1968
$10\frac{1}{2} \times 8\frac{1}{2}$

70. *Rebirth in the Western Sea*, 1968
$9\frac{3}{4} \times 7\frac{5}{8}$

71. *Plate 27*, 1969
$5\frac{1}{2} \times 4\frac{3}{4} \times \frac{1}{8}$

72. *Emblem of Infinity*, 1969
$4 \times 5\frac{1}{2}$

*73. *The Matrix*, 1970
$6\frac{1}{2} \times 8 \times 1\frac{1}{2}$

74. *Shining in Vacant Space*, 1975
$11\frac{1}{2} \times 9\frac{1}{8} \times 1$

75. *Adulterated Flag*, 1975
$7 \times 8\frac{3}{4}$

76. *Peach Hum with Threads*, 1979
$6\frac{1}{2} \times 7\frac{1}{2}$

77. *Peach Hum with Lines*, 1980
$6\frac{1}{2} \times 7\frac{1}{2}$

78. *Rose of Fire*, 1980
77×58
Collection Philip Morris Companies, Inc.
New York

79. *Manuscript Writing*, 1980
$7 \times 8\frac{3}{8}$

80. Untitled *(Eyes Series I)*, 1980
$9\frac{1}{2} \times 5\frac{3}{4}$

81. *O Crystalline Fount (Eyes Series II)*, 1982
$6\frac{3}{8} \times 6\frac{1}{4}$

82. Untitled, 1983
$5\frac{1}{2} \times 5\frac{3}{8}$

83. *The First Dust of Spring*, ca. 1984
$7\frac{1}{4} \times 6\frac{1}{8}$

84. *Your Glance Scatters Leaves*, ca. 1984
$4 \times 5\frac{3}{4}$

85. Untitled, 1985
$6\frac{5}{8} \times 7\frac{1}{2}$

86. *Schwitters' Smile*, 1985
7×9

87. *Creatures*, 1985
$4\frac{1}{4} \times 5\frac{5}{8} \times 1\frac{5}{8}$ (closed)

88. *Windows*, 1985
$5\frac{1}{4} \times 3\frac{3}{4} \times 2\frac{3}{4}$ (closed)

89. *The Via Sancta*, 1985
$35 \times 26\frac{1}{2} \times 4\frac{1}{8}$

90. *Upon a Grey Shore*, 1986
$41 \times 30\frac{1}{2} \times 6\frac{1}{4}$

91. *Far Off, Most Secret, Inviolate Rose*, 1986
$38 \times 25\frac{3}{4} \times 5\frac{1}{4}$

92. *The Flower Lies Hidden*, 1986
$27\frac{7}{8} \times 22\frac{1}{8} \times 6\frac{5}{8}$

*New York only
**New York and Chicago only
***Chicago only

93. *Hum,* ca. 1986
$74\frac{3}{8} \times 75\frac{3}{8}$

94. Collection of postcard collages, 1982–88
Approximately 4×6 each
Collection Katharine Kuh

95. Collection of postcard collages, 1968–81
Approximately 4×6 each
Collection The Cleveland Museum of Art
Gift of Katharine Kuh

96. Collection of postcard collages, 1966–86
Approximately 4×6 each
Collection Diana Epstein and Millicent Safro

ASSEMBLAGES

Like her collages, Tawney's assemblages contain a variety of found objects gathered over the years. Eggs, feathers, bones, and shells are infused with new meaning. Numbers 98 and 99 are box constructions inspired by the Jacquard loom. Numbers 112 and 113 are collage chests—each drawer a secret-bearing container—and numbers 119 through 121 are Tawney's unsittable collage chairs.

97. *And the Sound Is the Sound of the Sea,* 1964
$1\frac{3}{8} \times 8\frac{1}{2} \times 5\frac{1}{8}$

98. *Seed Puzzle on Three Levels,* 1966
$7\frac{7}{8} \times 5\frac{7}{8} \times 3\frac{1}{2}$

99. *Even Thread Had a Speech,* 1966
$5 \times 5\frac{1}{4} \times 2\frac{1}{4}$

100. *Médecins Anciens,* 1966
$2\frac{1}{2} \times 8\frac{1}{2} \times 5\frac{1}{4}$

101. *Bibliotheca Chemica,* 1966
$14 \times 12\frac{1}{4} \times 2\frac{3}{4}$
Private collection

102. *Materia Medica,* 1967
$2\frac{1}{4} \times 9\frac{1}{4} \times 5\frac{3}{4}$

103. *Feather Music,* ca. 1967
$5\frac{1}{2} \times 2 \times 4$

104. *Udjat,* 1968
$2 \times 7\frac{1}{4} \times 5\frac{1}{2}$

105. *These Words in Sand,* 1968
$2\frac{3}{4} \times 8\frac{1}{2} \times 5\frac{1}{8}$

*106. *Pia Avis,* 1969
$6\frac{1}{4} \times 6\frac{3}{8} \times 4\frac{3}{4}$

*107. *Time Trembling,* 1969
$6 \times 6\frac{1}{4} \times 4\frac{3}{4}$

108. *The Fairest of Plants,* 1969
$7 \times 7\frac{1}{4} \times 5\frac{1}{4}$

*109. *A Dry Cry from the Desert,* 1970
$9\frac{1}{2} \times 5\frac{1}{2} \times 4\frac{3}{4}$

110. *Birth,* 1970
$2 \times 10\frac{1}{8} \times 3\frac{1}{2}$

*111. *Dark Music,* ca. 1972–74
$9\frac{1}{4} \times 3\frac{3}{8} \times 6$

112. *Collage Chest II,* work in progress, begun 1974
$13\frac{1}{8} \times 5\frac{3}{8} \times 11\frac{1}{4}$

*113. *Collage Chest,* work in progress, begun 1974
$37\frac{1}{4} \times 21\frac{1}{4} \times 22$
Courtesy Helen Drutt Gallery
New York and Philadelphia

114. *Supreme,* begun ca. 1974, completed 1984
46×15
Collection Edna S. Beron

115. *Celestial Messenger,* 1978
$2\frac{1}{4} \times 5\frac{1}{4} \times 2\frac{1}{4}$

116. *Easter Breakfast,* 1982
$3\frac{1}{4} \times 7\frac{3}{4}$ diam.

117. *Wounded Duck,* 1984
$5\frac{3}{4} \times 14\frac{1}{8} \times 4$

118. *Foot Forms,* 1984–86
$2\frac{1}{4} \times 5\frac{1}{2} \times 2\frac{1}{4}$ each

119. *In Utero,* 1985
$48 \times 48 \times 48$

120. *Chariot*, 1985
    $26 \times 16\frac{1}{4} \times 15\frac{5}{8}$

121. *By the Secret Ladder*, ca. 1986
    $15\frac{3}{4} \times 5\frac{1}{4} \times 5\frac{1}{2}$

122. *Feather Music*, 1987
    $5\frac{3}{4} \times 2\frac{1}{2} \times 4$

123. *Feather Music*, 1987
    $3\frac{3}{8} \times 2 \times 4$

124. *Ode to a Sparrow*, 1987
    $8 \times 11\frac{7}{8} \times 3\frac{1}{4}$

125. *Or to an Illegible Stone*, 1989
    $3 \times 8\frac{3}{8} \times 7\frac{1}{4}$

*126. *Half Heard, in the Stillness*, 1989
    $4\frac{3}{4} \times 11\frac{1}{2} \times 5\frac{1}{8}$

*New York only
**New York and Chicago only
***Chicago only

Lenore Tawney in her Chicago studio, working on *Lost and Proud*, 1957.

Chronology

Compiled by KATHLEEN NUGENT MANGAN

1907   Born in Lorain, Ohio, daughter of Sarah Jennings and William Gallagher.

1927   Moves to Chicago.

1927–42   Works as proofreader for publisher of court opinions, and attends evening classes at Art Institute of Chicago.

1941   Marries George Tawney.

1943   Death of George Tawney. *36*

1943–45   Resides in Urbana, Illinois. Studies art at University of Illinois.

1945   Travels to Mexico.

1946   Returns to Chicago.

1946–47   Attends Institute of Design, Chicago. Studies sculpture with Alexander Archipenko, drawing with Laszlo Moholy-Nagy, drawing and watercolor painting with Emerson Woelffer, weaving with Marli Ehrman.

1947–48   Further studies with Archipenko in Chicago and at his studio in Woodstock, New York.

1949–51   Lives in Paris and travels extensively throughout Europe and North Africa.

1954   Studies tapestry with Martta Taipale at Penland School of Crafts, Penland, North Carolina.

1955   Begins open-warp weavings.

1956   Travels throughout Greece and Near East to Lebanon, Jordan, Syria, and Egypt.

1957   Tapestry commissioned by Marshall Field, North Shore Shopping Center, Chicago.

     Member, textile design panel, American Craftsmen's Council's (now American Craft Council) First National Conference of Craftsmen, Asilomar, California.

     Moves to 27 Coenties Slip, New York.

1958   Moves to 27 South Street, New York.

Lenore Tawney in her Coenties Slip studio, 1958.

1960	Completes tapestry commissioned by Interchurch Center, New York.	1976	Weaves *Waters above the Firmament,* her last work on the loom.
1961	Studies gauze weave with Lili Blumenau; explores gauze-weave techniques.	1976–77	Travels to India.
1962	Develops open reed and creates woven forms.	1977	Moves to Quakertown, New Jersey.

1960   Completes tapestry commissioned by Interchurch Center, New York.

1961   Studies gauze weave with Lili Blumenau; explores gauze-weave techniques.

1962   Develops open reed and creates woven forms.

Moves to Thomas Street, and then to Beekman Street, New York.

1963   Commission for ark veil, Congregation Solel, Highland Park, Illinois.

Travels to Peru and Bolivia.

Dark River (1962) acquired by Museum of Modern Art, New York.

1964   During First World Congress of Craftsmen, sponsored by American Craftsmen's Council in New York, visits New Jersey factory to see an industrial Jacquard loom.

Studies Jacquard harness at Textile Institute, Philadelphia.

Begins a series of drawings inspired by Jacquard loom.

1964–65   Begins work in collage and assemblage.

Makes first postcard collages.

1966   Moves to Spring Street, New York.

1969   Travels throughout Far East to Japan and Thailand, with extended stay in India.

1970   Meets Swami Muktananda.

Moves to East 4th Street, New York.

1973   Moves to Wooster Street, New York.

1974   Integrates weaving and paper collage.

1975   Elected Fellow of American Craftsmen's Council (inaugural group).

1976   Weaves *Waters above the Firmament,* her last work on the loom.

1976–77   Travels to India.

1977   Moves to Quakertown, New Jersey.

1977–78   Receives General Services Administration commission for lobby of Santa Rosa Federal Building, Santa Rosa, California. Creates and installs *Cloud Series IV.*

1978   Artist-in-residence, University of Notre Dame, Indiana.

1979   Receives National Endowment for the Arts Craftsman's Fellowship Grant.

1981   *Cloud Series VI* commissioned for Frank J. Lausche State Office Building, Cleveland.

Returns to New York.

1982   Artist-in-residence, Fabric Workshop, Philadelphia.

Travels to Taiwan and India.

1983   *Cloud Series VII* commissioned for Western Connecticut State University, Danbury.

Guest Lecturer for Visual Arts and Fiber, Banff Center for the Arts, Alberta, Canada.

Receives Honor Award for Outstanding Achievement in the Visual Arts, Women's Caucus for Art, Port of History Museum, Philadelphia.

Triune (1961) acquired by Metropolitan Museum of Art, New York.

Waters above the Firmament (1976) acquired by Art Institute of Chicago.

1987   Distinguished Lecturer, University of Arizona, Tucson.

Receives American Craft Council's Gold Medal.

Exhibition History

1 9 8 6   Mokotoff Gallery, New York.

1 9 8 8   Helen Drutt Gallery, New York.

1 9 9 0   "Lenore Tawney: A Retrospective,"
American Craft Museum, New York.
Tours nationally through July 1991.

SELECTED GROUP EXHIBITIONS

1 9 4 9   "International Textile Exhibition,"
University of North Carolina, Greensboro.

1 9 5 0   "Good Design," Merchandise Mart,
Chicago.

1 9 5 4   "Midwest Designer-Craftsmen,"
Art Institute of Chicago.

1 9 5 5   "Good Design," Museum of Modern
Art, New York.

1 9 5 6   "Craftsmanship in a Changing World,"
Museum of Contemporary Crafts (now
American Craft Museum) inaugural
exhibition, New York.

1 9 5 7   "Midwest Designer-Craftsmen,"
Art Institute of Chicago.

1 9 5 8   "American Artists and Craftsmen,"
American Pavilion, Brussels World's Fair.

1 9 6 1   "Director's Choice," Philadelphia
Museum of Art.

1 9 6 2   "Adventures in Art," Fine Arts Pavilion,
Seattle World's Fair.

1 9 6 3   "Woven Forms," Museum of
Contemporary Crafts, New York.

1 9 6 4   "Gewebte Formen,"
Kunstgewerbemuseum, Zurich.

"Triennale di Milano," Milan.

1 9 6 9   "Wall Hangings," Museum of
Modern Art, New York. Tours nationally
through December 1969.

"Objects USA," Johnson Collection of
Contemporary Crafts, assembled by
Johnson Wax. Premieres at National
Collection of Fine Arts, Washington,
D.C.; tours nationally and internationally.

1 9 7 4   "Nine Artists/Coenties Slip," Whitney
Museum of American Art, Downtown
Branch, New York.

"In Praise of Hands," Ontario Science
Center, Toronto.

1 9 7 5   "7ème Biennale Internationale de la
Tapisserie," Musée Cantonal des Beaux-
Arts, Lausanne.

1 9 7 7   "Fiberworks," Cleveland Museum of Art.

"Lenore Tawney and a Fiber Tradition,"
Kansas City Art Institute, Kansas City,
Missouri.

1 9 7 8   "Tawney/Higa/Sawada," Hunterdon Art
Center, Clinton, New Jersey.

1 9 7 9   "Form and Fiber, Works by Toshiko
Takaezu and Lenore Tawney," Cleveland
Institute of Art.

"100 Artists, 100 Years: Alumni of the
School of the Art Institute of Chicago
Centennial Exhibition," Art Institute of
Chicago.

"Weich und Plastisch: Soft-Art,"
Kunsthaus Zurich.

1 9 8 1   "Lenore Tawney/Toshiko Takaezu,"
Foster Gallery, University of Wisconsin,
Eau Claire.

"The Art Fabric: Mainstream," American
Federation of Arts. Premieres at San
Francisco Museum of Modern Art; tours
nationally through February 1984.

1983 "llème Biennale Internationale de la Tapisserie," Musée Cantonal des Beaux-Arts, Lausanne.

1986 "Fiber R/Evolution," Milwaukee Art Museum and University Art Museum, University of Wisconsin, Milwaukee. Tours nationally through June 1987.

"Craft Today: Poetry of the Physical," American Craft Museum, New York. Tours nationally through October 1988.

1987 "The Eloquent Object," Philbrook Museum of Art, Tulsa, Oklahoma. Tours nationally and internationally through February 1990.

1989 "Craft Today USA," American Craft Museum, New York. Premieres at the Musée des Arts Decoratifs, Paris; tours internationally through June 1992.

"Frontiers in Fiber: The Americans," North Dakota Museum of Art, Grand Forks. Premieres at Ishikawa Design Center, Kanazawa, Japan; tours internationally through November 1990.

"Fiber Concepts," Arizona State University Art Museum, Tempe.

Installation of weavings by Lenore Tawney, Benson Gallery, Bridgehampton, New York, 1967.

Selected Bibliography

BOOKS

Albers, Anni. *On Weaving*. Middletown, Connecticut: Wesleyan University Press, 1965.

Constantine, Mildred, and Jack Lenor Larsen. *The Art Fabric: Mainstream*. New York: Van Nostrand Reinhold, 1981.

————. *Beyond Craft: The Art Fabric*. New York: Van Nostrand Reinhold, 1972.

Kaufmann, Ruth. *The New American Tapestry*. New York: Reinhold Book Corporation, 1968.

Kuenzi, André. *La Nouvelle Tapisserie*. Lausanne: Bibliothèque des Arts, 1981.

Munro, Eleanor. *Originals: American Women Artists*. New York: Simon and Schuster, 1979.

Nordness, Lee. *Objects: USA*. New York: Viking Press, 1970.

Rubinstein, Charlotte Streifer. *American Women Artists*. Boston: G.K. Hall and Company, 1982.

Thalacker, Donald W. *The Place of Art in the World of Architecture*. New York: Chelsea House Publishers, 1980.

Epître (detail), 1967, 7" × 7¾" × 1¼".

PERIODICALS

Adams, Alice. "Lenore Tawney." *Craft Horizons* 22 (January/February 1962): 39.

Barron, Stephanie. "Giving Art History the Slip." *Art in America* 62 (March/April 1974): 80–84.

Henry, Gerrit. "Cloudworks and Collage." *Art In America* 74 (June 1986): 116–21.

Hoff, Margo. "Lenore Tawney: The Warp Is Her Canvas." *Craft Horizons* 17 (November/December 1957): 14–19.

Howard, Richard. "Tawney." *Craft Horizons* 31 (February 1975): 46–47, 71–72.

Kuh, Katharine. "Sculpture: Woven and Knotted." *Saturday Review* 51 (July 27, 1968): 36–37.

Larsen, Jack Lenor. "Lenore Tawney—Inspiration to Those Who Want To Develop Their Artistic Potential." *House Beautiful* 104 (March 1962): 160–61, 175–77.

"Lenore Tawney: Her Designs Show Imaginative Departure from Traditional Tapestry Techniques." *Handweaver and Craftsman* 13 (Spring 1962): 6–9.

Orenstein, Gloria. "Lenore Tawney: The Craft of the Spirit." *The Feminist Art Journal* 2 (Winter 1973–74): 11–13.

Orth, Maureen. "The Cosmic Creations of Lenore Tawney." *New York Woman* 1 (May/June 1987): 66–67.

Park, Betty. "Lenore Tawney." *Craft Horizons* 38 (October 1978): 52.

Schorr, Mimi. "Fiber Sculpture." *Saturday Review* 55 (May 20, 1972): 57–61.

Schuyler, James. "Lenore Tawney." *Craft Horizons* 27 (November/December 1967): 20–25.

Slivka, Rose. "The New Tapestry." *Craft Horizons* 23 (March/April 1963): 10–19, 48–49.

Smith, Dido. "Lenore Tawney." *Craft Horizons* 30 (August 1970): 54.

Winter, Amy. "Lenore Tawney." *Arts* 60 (January 1986): 108.

EXHIBITION CATALOGUES

ONE-PERSON EXHIBITIONS

Lenore Tawney, 1961, Staten Island Museum, New York, text by James Coggin and Agnes Martin.

Lenore Tawney, 1975, California State University, Fullerton, text by Dextra Frankel, Bernard Kester, and Katharine Kuh.

Lenore Tawney: A Personal World, 1978, Brookfield Craft Center, Connecticut, preface and interview with Lenore Tawney by Jean d'Autilia.

Lenore Tawney, 1979, New Jersey State Museum, Trenton, text by Katharine Kuh and Leah P. Sloshberg.

GROUP EXHIBITIONS

Woven Forms, 1963, Museum of Contemporary Crafts, New York, introduction by Paul J. Smith, text by Ann Wilson.

Wall Hangings, 1969, The Museum of Modern Art, New York, introduction by Mildred Constantine and Jack Lenor Larsen.

Nine Artists/Coenties Slip, 1974, Whitney Museum of American Art Downtown Branch, New York.

Fiberworks, 1977, Cleveland Museum of Art, foreword by Sherman E. Lee, preface by Edward B. Henning, text by Evelyn Svec Ward.

Weich und Plastisch: Soft-Art, 1979, Kunsthaus Zurich, Switzerland, foreword by Erika Billeter, text by Magdalena Abakanowicz, Erika Billeter, Mildred Constantine, Richard Paul Lohse, Willy Rotzler, and André Thomkins.

Fiber R/Evolution, 1986, Milwaukee Art Museum and University Art Museum, University of Wisconsin, Milwaukee, foreword by Russell Bowman, text by Jane Fassett Brite and Jean Stamsta, and John Perreault.

The Eloquent Object, 1987, Philbrook Museum of Art, Tulsa, Oklahoma, edited by Marcia Manhart and Tom Manhart, text by George L. Aguirre, Jonathan L. Fairbanks, Penelope Hunter-Stiebel, Mary Jane Jacob, Horace Freeland Judson, Ronda Kasl, Lucy L. Lippard, Marcia Manhart and Tom Manhart, John Perreault, Rose Slivka, and Edwin L. Wade.

Fiber Concepts, 1989, Arizona State University Art Museum, Tempe, text by Lucinda H. Gedeon.

About the Authors

KATHLEEN NUGENT MANGAN has worked extensively as a curator of contemporary craft. Curator at the American Craft Museum from 1981 to 1985, Mangan was responsible for many exhibitions including "The Handmade Paper Book" and "Art to Wear: New Handmade Clothing." She is now an independent curator. Mangan has lectured at museums throughout the country and contributed to many catalogues and publications dedicated to contemporary textiles and other craft media.

KATHARINE KUH is a critic and consultant known for her myriad contributions to the history of twentieth-century art. From 1942 to 1959, she was curator of modern art at the Art Institute of Chicago and from 1959 to 1977, she served as art editor of the *Saturday Review*. Among her many publications are *Art Has Many Faces, The Artist's Voice, Break-Up: The Core of Modern Art,* and *The Open Eye.*

As president of the Biennale de la Tapisserie in Lausanne, Switzerland, ERIKA BILLETER has been a pivotal figure in the avant garde of contemporary textiles. Her contribution to their history has included many exhibitions, among them the groundbreaking "Weich und Plastisch: Soft-Art" presented in 1978 at the Kunsthaus in Zurich. Billeter is currently director of the Musée Cantonal des Beaux-Arts in Lausanne.

PAUL J. SMITH, director emeritus of the American Craft Museum, is himself a pioneer figure in the craft and design field. Director of the American Craft Museum from 1963 to 1987, he organized innumerable exhibitions on contemporary craft including the museum's inaugural show "Craft Today: Poetry of the Physical" in 1986 and most recently "Craft Today: USA" currently on tour in Europe.

Photography Credits

Illustrations have been supplied and are reproduced by kind permission of the following:

David Attie: pgs. 31 (bottom), 150; The Art Institute of Chicago: pgs. 28 (bottom), 77; Ferdinand Boesch: pgs. 6, 25 (right), 26, 27, 40; Barbeau Engh: pgs. 31, 32, 33; George Erml: color photography, all journal entries, and black-and-white photographs on pgs. 9, 44, 51, 55, 58, 59, 63, 130, 131, 134, 135, 138, 139, 156; Nancy Finn: pgs. 18 (bottom), 46, 47; Yousuf

Karsh: frontispiece; Kunstgewerbemuseum Zurich: pg. 42; Nina Leen, Life Magazine © 1966 Time Inc.: pg. 16; The Metropolitan Museum of Art: pg. 24; Clayton J. Price: pgs. 10, 28 (top), 155; Joyce Pomeroy Schwartz: pg. 35 (bottom); Aaron Siskind: pgs. 20 (top), 149; Paul J. Smith: pgs. 12, 14, 15; John Bigelow Taylor, NYC: pg. 141.

The American Craft Museum wherever possible has made every effort to contact the photographers.